Thought Leaders

W9-BPM-493

# Connected
# Schools

The Cisco Internet Business Solutions Group (IBSG) helps customers transform their institutions and organisations (or business), create new services, and drive industry-leading change through the use of technology and process innovation. IBSG consultants offer a unique combination of in-depth industry, business, and technical knowledge. The IBSG Public Sector Practice works with large, complex entities in Europe, the Middle East, Africa, Asia/Pacific, Americas International and the United States, giving its consultants a broad and deep global perspective.

The ISBG Public Service Practice work as trusted advisors at the most senior levels of large public-sector organisations where transformation is imminent or there is the potential for groundbreaking projects likely to be emulated by others. These projects include education, tax, and payment systems along with mass client service and claims processing organisations. Other projects range from integrated justice and security initiatives, large procurement operations as well as whole-government programmes and those seeking seamless government and transformed service delivery across their full range of services.

Published by
**Premium Publishing**
27 Bassein Park Road
London
W12 9RW
creastanorris@btconnect.com

First published 2004

Copyright © 2004 Premium Publishing
The moral rights of the authors have been asserted.
All rights reserved.

Without limiting the rights under copyright reserved
above, no part of this publication may be reproduced,
stored or introduced into a retrieval system or
transmitted in any form or by any means without
the prior knowledge and written permission of the
copyright owner and the above publisher of the book.

ISBN 0-9546445-5-7

Edited by Michelle Selinger
Design by Loman Street Studio
Cover Images by Getty Images
Printed by G&B printers

A catalogue record for this book is available from
the British Library

# Contents

# Contents

# Introduction

# Introduction

**Michelle Selinger** | Executive Adviser Education, Cisco Systems EMEA.

## The advance of the Knowledge Society

This collection of essays and interviews encapsulates some of the most innovative and exciting visions in worldwide education policy and practice today. The essays in this book are from those who are visionaries in their field. They include the perspectives of the very advanced as well as from those in countries that are just embarking on the journey towards connected education. All can learn from each other and late starters can catch up fast and innovate intelligently, influenced by the thoughts, ideas and experiences represented in this volume.

Education has always been one of the primary drivers for economic growth, peace and prosperity. Increasingly we are living in a Knowledge Society, in which connectivity allows us access to all kinds of information at unprecedented speed and in multiple formats. Access to this information and to the tools required to achieve it are growing fast. The same trends are leading to the possibility of new forms of education which will empower the children of today to take an active role in developing the shape and direction of their society. At the same time, research into the functioning of the brain, different learning styles and new pedagogies[1] is growing fast and this has led to widescale implementation of changes to education systems while focusing attention on improving pedagogy.

1. For example: Bruner, J. (1996) The Culture of Education: Cambridge, MA. Greenfield, S. Harvard University Press; (2000) Brain Story: Why Do We Think and Feel as We Do? London: BBC Consumer Publishing. Gardner, H. (1993) frames of Mind: Multiple Intelligences. New York: Basic Books

Governments across the world are focusing more and more resources on the development of their educational systems. The World Declaration on Education for All was adopted by governments in 1990 in Jomtien, Thailand. It highlights education as one of the most important factors in global development, peace and security in the twenty-first century and sets ambitious targets for 2015 which were reaffirmed in Dakar in 2000 by the World Education Forum. Good primary education is known to have a positive impact on lower fertility rates, better diets and the earlier and more effective diagnosis of illness. The link between literacy and life expectancy is strong. Worldwide governments, individual policy-makers and ministries of education are on the cusp of making enormous changes and information and communications technology is heralded as the prime driver. School districts, regional and local education authorities and school principals are experimenting with new curricula, pedagogy and assessment systems; and teachers and their students are collectively creating new ways of working within and beyond the classroom.

'Connected schools provide new opportunities to improve the learning experience and to meet the challenges of today's Knowlege Society.'
MICHELLE SELINGER

The Internet has caused an explosion of access to information on a global level, which has only served to highlight the fact that no teacher can possibly know it all – and why should they? It is now recognised that a complete paradigm shift is necessary in the way that schools operate within society. We cannot jeopardise our children's future by using outdated methods of teaching. We need to take advantage of developments in technology to secure an education that is relevant and responsive to the needs of society as it evolves. Teaching and learning need to be shaped in a different way, with more personalisation, individualisation and localisation. There needs to be less focus on a narrow curriculum. There needs to be development of innovative assessment methods that really test for understanding and application rather than just factual recall. We need to teach learners how to locate relevant information and judge the credibility of their sources. They need to learn how to think critically and to solve problems, how to communicate at all levels with a diverse range of people and how to take responsibility for how and what they learn. Connected schools create the possibilities for changing pedagogy and provide new opportunities to improve the learning experience, so that our children and our societies are ready to meet the challenges of today's Knowledge Society.

### The slow revolution

Recently I had a conversation with a friend with whom I used to teach some years ago. Now a deputy head in a UK school with a half-time teaching load, she told me that her school was installing interactive whiteboards in all its classrooms. 'It makes so much difference,' she said. 'If it's there you will use it, but if you have to lug a laptop and a projector into each classroom you teach in, then you won't bother – by the time you've set it up and got it working much of the lesson time has gone.' We agreed that technology has to be accessible, reliable and ubiquitous if it really is going to have the impact that has been predicted for some 20 years, when the first microcomputers began to appear in schools.

ICT as a catalyst for radical educational change has long been predicted by visionaries such as Papert, Turkle and Castells. There have been significant changes in education: certainly the curriculum has become more relevant, assessment strategies have broadened and teaching styles are more varied. But the layout and design of schools and the structure of the curriculum have changed very little in all but a relatively few places. The introduction of digital resources and Internet technology may have improved the quality of the learning experience but the teacher is still the coordinator of the learning and the director of what shall be learnt in what order and when. Students have little freedom in schools to go beyond the statutory curriculum and to pursue interests in depth.

2. Cuban, L. (2001) Oversold and Underused: Computers in the Classroom. Boston: Harvard University Press.

3. Cox, M. and Abbott, C. (eds) (2004) A Review of the Research Literature Relating to ICT and Attainment. A Report for the DFES. Coventry, Becta. Available at: http://www.becta.org.uk/ page_documents/research/ ict_attainment04.pdf

Larry Cuban[2] argues that teachers will appropriate any technology to do what they have always done. And why should they change? If the teaching methods they have always known and used provide the results that they and education authorities are seeking, then there is little reason to transform their teaching. Some dissonance is needed; some ripples that will create the catalyst for change to ensure that schools recognise individual achievement and learning styles and provide every learner with the opportunity to succeed. Technology provides the tools to do this and the evidence suggests they are effective.[3] But evidence is hard to measure systematically when students only have access to technology on a sporadic basis; when PCs are kept in computer rooms and visited only occasionally, and when access is not complete and universal.

Cuban describes a 'slow revolution' in which, on the one hand, many teachers are increasingly adopting the technology but are doing so in a way that ensures that they continue to do what they did before; while, on the other hand, other teachers are using the technology to transform their classrooms into student-centred, active learning places. These latter teachers are at the vanguard of a movement that may eventually have profound consequences.

### Structure of the book

The book is divided into four sections; the first section focuses on teachers and learners; the second on practical frameworks; the third on policy frameworks; while the fourth reflects on changes to date and considers possibilities for the future. The themes covered vary from the changing role of teachers, bringing students to centre stage, curriculum and assessment developments, the electronic content debate and the place of schools in society. All this is set within the context of broadband deployment to schools, home and community, and with the associated tools to facilitate communication, collaboration and access to dynamic, interactive resources and environments. These will enable the personalisation and individualisation of learning necessary to produce the society and workforce of tomorrow, combined with the essential critical thinking and problem-solving skills required for life in the twenty-first century.

### Teachers and learners

#### Learners' views of schooling

Putting the essay by the two young learners at the beginning of the book was an easy decision: today's learners are the workforce (and teachers) of tomorrow. They have grown up with technology around them. Most 18-year-olds in the developed world will have little memory of a life before mobile phones and PCs. For them the Internet is a given and a world without ubiquitous communication tools is incomprehensible. Surely learners' views of schooling and how it accords with the rest of their lives is of vital importance to policy-makers? It might even reduce disaffection, disruption and truancy in schools. Craig Jones and Kevin Smith have a compelling and inspiring story to tell. If we are to get the real change in education that everyone is predicting, we have to listen to the learners and involve them in decisions about what the school of tomorrow could look like and what activities should take place inside.

Craig and Kevin resent the way teachers control the learning environment and take decisions and empowerment away from students. Shirley Alexander in her essay points out that, even as young as eight, students do not want easy questions to answer. They want to think for themselves and come up with their own complex questions. Surely giving students the space to do this in school time is motivating and prepares them for life and work in which complex problems will face them all the time? Additionally, text no longer has to be the main medium for conveying meaning as it was in the age of books. Now sound, graphics, video and animation are equally and sometimes more effectively able to demonstrate and develop understanding. They also provide learners with more tools and more choices about how to obtain and convey meaning. Charles Handy, speaking in 2001[4], espoused his view of a more appropriate tertiary education, but his view can also be true of schools, as both the essays by Craig and Kevin and Shirley Alexander suggest. 'The curriculum would be arranged around a preponderance of open projects, with no predetermined correct solution, projects preferably anchored in real situations outside the classroom. These projects should be carried out in teams, and wherever possible those teams should be mixed sets of skills and backgrounds. It is critical that the young learn to work together and to appreciate the range of talents and skills that are both available and necessary to get anything done. The role of networked learning here can be immeasurable. Students will need a preponderance of resources from which to draw, discuss and debate in order to come to a solution or set of solutions. Schools need to prepare students for such further education and the workplace.'

4. Handy, C. (2001) Education for a New World. Available at http://www.nec.ac.uk/info/news -item?news_item_id=100437

No commentator suggests the abolition of schooling; they all see the social and communal nature of schools as essential to the development of the citizen. Teachers too are still perceived to be a crucial aspect of schooling, and although their role will change and develop, they are just as important in helping students learn how to learn as they were before the advent of technology. Michael Young, the founder of the UK Open University, saw teachers as educational companions; they accompanied students on part of their learning journey through life. The stress is on *accompanying* rather than *leading*. Accompanying suggests a partnership and a dialogue, providing guidance rather than making decisions for the learner. Perhaps with the increased personalisation and individualisation of learning, we can return to a Socratic dialogue between novices and experts in a mass education system rather than in one where education was for the privileged minority – a sort of

5. Selinger, M. and Gibson, I. (2004) Cultural Relevance and Technology use: Ensuring the Transformational Power of Learning Technologies in Culturally Defined Learning Environments. Proceedings of EdMedia 2004, Lugano, Switzerland, 22–26 June.

6. Willis, S. Johnston, P. Badger M. and Stewart-Weeks, M. (2004) The Connected Republic, San Jose: Cisco Systems.

'retro-progress'.[5] Just as the Athenian concept of the Republic as a polis run by all its citizens is at the heart of the concept of the connected republic[6], so the Socratic notion of the partnership between student and learner and the *immanence* of knowledge is at the heart of the connected school. One of the significant features of dialogue is that it emphasises collective, as opposed to solitary, activity. It is through the to and fro of argument among friends that understanding grows or is revealed. Networked learning facilitates such dialogue through a host of channels that were not available at the time of the ancient Greeks, and enables teacher and learners to meet in virtual time and space in addition to traditional classrooms and tutorials.

---

### 'Providing education to the community can ensure that a real learning community is forged in which everyone benefits.'

---

Another metaphor for the classroom is an orchestra where the teacher is the conductor. The students have all learnt to play their instruments; they each play the instrument they feel most comfortable with and which reveals their particular talents. They learn to play new tunes but build on their experience of playing, so that each new learning builds on what they already know and the tunes they play can be more complex and introduce new skills. Practice in the use of new skills is important if the orchestra is to play in harmony, each member making an important contribution, however easy or challenging their instrument. Primary school becomes the place where students first learn to play a range of instruments and find out where their particular talents lie; and secondary school is where they develop their skills in one or more instruments and learn to play in the orchestra.

### The importance of community

The essay from the two UK head teachers Marian Brooks and Eddie Brady is evidence of the importance of vision and leadership in schools, a fact also recognised by the Federation of Internet Education in Russia. Whatever the vision of a ministry of education or a region, it is head teachers who will drive change into the schools; support their staff and juggle resources in order to provide the best learning environment for their students. They have to believe in the role that networked technology can play in improving the quality of teaching and learning in their schools. For Brooks and Brady the home-school link is a crucial element to the success of learners. By involving and engaging parents and the community in the learning process students avoid isolation, and the boundaries between school, home and the community begin to blur. Brooks explains how this in turn has an impact on students' interest in learning and has produced results well above those expected in a school with such a high turnover of students. Learning becomes part of the whole day, not something that only goes on in school hours.

John Seely Brown and Paul Duguid argue in favour of communities in developing understanding and that knowledge comes from sharing experiences and information and ICT can support that.

---

'Education has only just begun to understand and translate into curricula on an appreciable scale. The reality that knowledge rather than being found in books and in lectures or on the Internet, is actually constructed in collaborations among learners. It is when technology supports the jerky, jagged, and looping lines of shared discovery that it fulfills its own evolutionary promise.'[7]

7. Brown, J.S & Duguid, P. (2002) The Social Life of Information, Cambridge: Harvard Business School

---

Access to the Internet and connecting home to school are important factors in maintaining interest and motivation, and Eddie Brady describes how he wants to make use of the 100Mbs link he has to the school to provide access at little or no cost to the surrounding homes of his students and their parents. The family income in the school catchment area is way below the national average, and few homes have connectivity. However, low-income families may have low levels of literacy or language barriers. Access to the Internet, may not mean accessibile or relevant content is available. Providing education to the community can ensure that a real learning community is forged in which everyone benefits; the school achieves better results, literacy levels are improved, learners are motivated and employment prospects and aspirations are raised. With this kind of thinking, the French Ministry of Education have adopted a plan to provide free Internet access points that will offer ICT training programmes and encourage access to the most disadvantaged. Their belief is that citizens can use these centres to promote a balanced discussion of the Internet and demonstrate the advantages connectivity can bring if it is used wisely.

The theme of community is apparent throughout many of these essays. John English describes the learning experience of students in Fairfax County in the US, a county renowned for its forward thinking about learning and its use of ICT to support it. Communities of learners and the involvement of parents and communities of teachers are all strong themes in Fairfax. At the same time personalisation and individualisation of learning is at the heart of their development. One of the innovative features in Fairfax's uses of ICT is that learning resources are produced by teachers within the county, and commercial resources are rarely used. These resources are made openly available and they have created a demand for subjects that would normally not be provided, such as Arabic as a foreign language. This gives an indication of how curriculum might develop in the future, through a community need rather than a national dictate.

The importance of home–school links is echoed yet again by Mark Edwards, superintendent of schools in Enrico County, Virginia in the US. He describes how the county is developing systems to ensure that parents are kept regularly informed of students' progress. Administration systems to deal with such a wealth of information are becoming more sophisticated, and 'data warehouses' are being developed on both sides of the Atlantic. English also discusses Internet security and argues that parents are the best filter as long as they are actively involved in monitoring their children and teaching them how to make independent decisions about their use of the Net.

## What should be learnt and how?

The move to personalisation and individualisation is another theme echoed throughout these essays. This is not the individualised learning of the 1970s and 80s that marred so much mathematics teaching, for example, nor the individualised learning systems of the 1990s, which had mixed success. In these scenarios students worked alone on individual tasks with little discussion or mutual support. The rhetoric behind individualisation and personalisation today is more about being able to tailor learning to meet the needs of each student, taking account of learning styles and learning preferences and allowing students to pursue their studies with a range of resources tailored to their individual needs and interests. It does not imply working in isolation, unless that is what a learner needs to do at a particular time. Sometimes it may be important to withdraw from a group to collect your thoughts, work on a problem or reflect on what you have learnt so far, and then to return to challenge and question in order to further your understanding. Lyle Oberg says, 'You have to grab a learner and play with their skills'; all learners need to be challenged whatever their abilities, and this implies giving them choices about where and how to learn, while David Miliband believes personallised learning is *the* debate in education today.'

ICT is the enabler providing students with access to a wealth of information: they can choose to learn from a mix of media, work with others within their school, in other schools, and with experts in the field using the Internet to transcend time and space. As John English says in his essay, it's about 'student-driven learning', a thought echoed by the two learners, Craig and Kevin. This notion is important to Eddie Brady, who wants to move away from subject-based learning and focus more on the learning process so that content becomes a vehicle through which young people become expert learners. For similar reasons Lyle Oberg also sees a blurring of subject boundaries.

The language in which content is presented is an issue for many countries, particularly those with minority languages and where the market is not large enough to support either content development or translations. It is recognised that the language of the Internet is predominantly English and in Hungary, as Ádám Horváth explains, European funding has been used to develop content for re-use across Europe. However, not all of it will be in Hungarian and Horváth argues that sometimes learning a language through learning a subject can be very effective. There is certainly other research evidence to support this assertion,[8] and now that the Internet is opening up the possibilities for learning beyond the classroom and providing the opportunity to learn from online courses, this theory can be increasingly put to the test and the research base developed. Existing research[9] has also shown that even when content is available in the home language, if it has been developed elsewhere then the cultural references and the pedagogical nuances may still make the materials less than fully effective.

The digitisation of content needs to be imaginative if it is to encourage learning. Ulf Lundin describes a discussion on the European SchoolNet about the development of learning objects within the framework of a project called Celebrate. This brings together ministries, content providers, and research organisations such as universities to look at and develop learning objects and makes them available to schools as a basis for pilot work. As the wealth of content has grown, meta-tagging has become an increasingly important factor in helping teachers and students to search for and find relevant information quickly and efficiently. In the Netherlands, Toine Maes explains how they have gone one step beyond that and started to examine and develop the whole content chain moving into a concept of 'content stimulation'.

8. See for example Collier, V.P. (1995) Acquiring a Second Language for School. Directions in Language & Education. National Clearinghouse for Bilingual Education, 1(4).

9. Selinger, M. (2004) The cultural and pedagogical implications of a global e-learning programme Cambridge Journal of Education, 34(2), 213-239.

---

## 'Exactly what are the parameters of "good" e-content? Who determines how content is packaged?'

---

Flexibility in national curricula is increasingly possible. In Alberta, Canada, Lyle Oberg, the Minster of Learning, explains that only 65 per cent of the curriculum is standardised, while the remainder is flexible and at the discretion of the school. It can therefore be tailored to local and community needs. There are currently 1,500 courses available to high-school students. The best teachers in a specialist subject, or in subjects for which there is a shortage of teachers, will soon be able to teach across the province through the planned installation of video-conferencing suites in schools. This use of video technology can also be extended to invite adults other than teachers such as invited specialists from museums, art galleries, space centres etc to work with a class anywhere in the world where there is connectivity.

The essays in this book show that there is no clear consensus about the development of e-content. In fact the whole content debate is full of contradictions and questions. Exactly what are the parameters of 'good' content? Who are and should be the content developers? Who determines how content is packaged and whether the packages are suitable for all students however they learn? How much assessment should be built in and what form should it take? What degree of flexibility should the content include so that teachers can adapt it for their students or so students can select an appropriate path through the learning materials? Should collaboration and communication form part of a content 'solution' and what tools do we use? What happens to the new content created from these exchanges, and how should intellectual property issues be dealt with? How should learning objects be collated and tagged and what support should there be for teachers and learners to make best use of them? What flexibility is included for cross-subject work and thematic approaches to learning? As discussed earlier, Shirley Alexander's research indicated that we should work closely with students from the outset and give them a major role in the development of relevant content.

Assessment is also key in any curricula developments and David Miliband empasises this as a key theme in UK policy. He elaborates on the range of assesment tools that provide students with formative feedback and support individual learning goals. Eddie Brady also sees assessment in terms of students being able to demonstrate what they know and can do in a range of ways facilitated by ICT.

### Developing policies and frameworks

Ulf Lundin, Director of the European SchoolNet (EUN), describes the phases any government has to take into account when planning an ICT in education strategy, and how EUN supports and promotes their efforts. He explains that many countries are still in the first phase of computer installation and teacher training. Those in the second phase are beginning to evaluate the use made of the technologies to date, and the third phase, which he sees as most challenging, requires the re-evaluation and examination of how these technologies can be put to more effective use.

10. Rodgers, E.M. (2003) Diffusion of Innovations. 5th edn. New York: Free Press.

In his book *Diffusion of Innovations*[10] Everett Rogers examines the rate of adoption of innovations and what hinders or accelerates a new idea. Rogers talks about how the idea of a laptop computer was dismissed by Toshiba as a fad; the engineer who had the original idea went against the company and developed a prototype secretly in Japan. When it was still rejected by the board, he presented it to an executive for Toshiba Europe, who had the vision to see its potential. Today laptop computers, together with wireless access, are the 'killer' tools that will transform education because of the accessibility and ubiquity they provide. John Anderson and Jimmy Stewart from Northern Ireland have seen the sudden spiralling of innovation within schools over the past few years; the rate of adoption has taken time and it is only by providing increased access, reliability and support that this has been able to happen. More reliable networks and computers have also made a difference in both teachers' attitudes to technology and the extent to which they integrate it into their teaching, but it has been giving each teacher a laptop computer that has been the single factor that has made the most significant difference and clearly indicates how a policy decision can have such a clear impact on the implementation and development of a strategy.

As later adopters, emerging and developing nations are able to benefit from the hindsight of implementation of innovation in the developed world. This is apparent in the essay from Ádám Horváth, IT adviser to the Minister of Education in Hungary, where both the Government's vision and associated development plans have been able to examine the experience of early adopters and take account of all the false steps and lessons learnt, as well as the success factors in planning a coherent strategy that will accelerate the deployment and integration of ICT into Hungarian schools.

---

'More reliable networks and computers have made a difference in teachers' attitudes to technology and the extent to which they integrate it into their teaching.'

---

The essay from Alexander Yu Uvarov from the Scientific Council of Cybernetics at the Russian Academy of sciences in Moscow is a reflective piece that examines how the impact of computers, ICT and the 'informatisation' of education have influenced discussion of reform in Russian education, and explores how ICT and the Internet can challenge and open up education in the country. He demonstrates that leadership and vision by governments are as important as funding. The UK Government, for example, has made and continues to make a huge investment in ICT in schools and has implemented a range of initiatives to direct and shape the implementation of technology in UK schools.

At the annual BETT conference in January 2004 Charles Clarke, Secretary of State for Education, informed the audience that a further £700 million pounds would be invested in ICT in the UK by 2006. David Miliband explains in his essay the main goals this investment will support. It is interesting to draw parallels between the UK, France and Hungary – there are many similarities in the visions and specific medium term goals which frame their countries policies. The extent of investment needed by the Government for implementation of infrastructure to enable Internet connectivity and student–PC ratios that will ensure the environment can sustain the changes envisioned cannot be underestimated. But the infrastructure is only one part of the equation: teacher training, curriculum and attitudes to learners are of equal importance.

Any investment in educational technology needs to be set in the context of the economic needs and aspirations of the country. In Jordan the investment has been supported by a strong public–private partnership initiative based on a government strategy for the economy that encompasses education as one of the central drivers for change. Jordan has a very young population (over 35 per cent of the population is under the age of 15), and it has few natural resources, so it has decided that its future economic growth depends on the development of a Knowledge Economy. Under the visionary leadership of King Abdullah II, Jordan has established an ambitious programme called the Education Reform for the Knowledge Economy (ERfKE). The Jordan Education Initiative, described in the essay by Emile Cubeisy and Andreas Cox, was initiated in May 2003 in an attempt to accelerate the vision though public–private partnerships with international and local companies. Jordan is building capacity through innovative partnerships and thought leadership from experts from around the World. Their vision is predicated on a belief in helping to build a world based on mutual understanding – their determination, inspiration and execution have much to teach us all.

### Teacher training

Teacher training and professional development are crucial to the success of any technology innovations in schools. In Russia an award-winning programme was started in 2000 by the Federation of Internet Education. In an ambitious plan they have set up 41 centres to train teachers in all aspects of ICT in education and soon expect over 100,000 teachers to have graduated from their courses – an average of 25,000 teachers a year. The extent of the training requirements is enormous as there are over 1.7 million teachers in Russia, so the cascading of training is going to be a very important factor in ensuring that every teacher begins to understand the ways in which Internet technologies can support teaching and learning.

In France only 20 per cent of teachers use multimedia in their lessons and this is of concern. With a large turnover of staff envisaged in the next six years the plan is to speed up training of the young teachers who will 'take up the baton'.

Toine Maes sums up the essence of teachers learning to use the technology; he sees it as the change from 'learning to use' to 'using to learn'. He believes that teachers will start to use ICT in their teaching once they are inspired by 'brilliant content'. Hence one of the main focuses of Kennisnet: the Netherlands education portal is the development of content and a tailor-made search engine or 'findengine' (Davindi) which provides a manageable number of qualified and précised links that do not daunt teachers or students.

As Kevin and Craig say of school, 'if they [teachers] are learning with us as well it might have a better sense of community'. Lyle Oberg has taken up this challenge and encouraged the teachers in Alberta to become researchers and to come up with ways to improve schools and student achievement.

Manfred Wolf from the Central Institute for Teacher Training and Staff Development in Germany reminds us that for this to function well, teachers need to feel confident that the technology will be reliable and not fail at a critical moment. He has devised the net@school project to ensure a reliable network in schools and teachers or technicians available at all times to troubleshoot and maintain the infrastructure.

David Miliband emphasises that teachers too need individualised learning and wants every teacher to identify their own development goals. Teachers as learners is a strong motivator for the development of the learning school.

### The school of tomorrow

What will innovative schools look like as we move into the next decade of the twenty-first century? Drawing on thought leaders in this book and beyond, it seems they will have similar structures to today. Perhaps age-related and grade-related classes, which Ulf Lundin sees as inhibitors of change, will have disappeared. Students will work together in teams in cross-curricular groups; and the borders between home and school will increasingly disappear. Lyle Oberg, like the other authors, believes that learners still need to go to school but that it will be the socialisation aspects of schools that will be the most important feature. Schools will also become community learning hubs which reach out to the community in an open and inviting way. Computer labs will become relics of the past, but computers will be available in tutor-supported, open learning areas, together with library facilities and other resources that students and the community need for independent research and study. Access will be provided around the clock.

'Computer labs will become relics of the past, but computers will be available in tutor-supported, open learning areas.'

Every teacher will be given a laptop with some sort of projection facility. If sufficient resources are not available to provide every student with a laptop, then there will be clusters of PCs or mobile labs with portable computers on a wireless trolley. If a group of students need to sit round a PC and work together, then they can do that in their own classroom without having to go elsewhere. There will also be lecture theatres for talks to large groups; classrooms where it's impossible for teachers to take centre stage; small group rooms and quiet rooms – all equipped with desktop PCs and/or wireless access.

David Triggs, Principal of Greensward College in the UK, sees schools becoming 'networked virtual organisations', and he describes a model in which world-class learning outcomes will be placed at the centre of the process and students will be taught to become 'global citizens'. He builds a circular model in which the school and community make up the next layer, partnership the third and the results the fourth.

In his essay, Ulf Lundin, who was previously a Minister of Education in Sweden, reflects on how the experience he has seen across Europe has led him to consider what he might do now if he were still Minister of Education. This includes:

• reviewing the institutional, curricular and evaluation framework to create a more flexible learning environment for students;
• placing the networked school at the centre;

- encouraging teachers to become more collaborative as the notion of one teacher alone in a classroom becomes a relic of the past;
- placing less emphasis on summative assessment, which is currently locking schools into a rigid curriculum structure.

The vision for the future of the connected school is perhaps best summed up in the essay by French Minister of Education, Francois Fillon, when he predicts: 'The school we want for tomorrow will be integrated into its local and international environment and open to the world, to its history, geography, cultures and people. It will be a school that facilitates dialogue between the generations, cultures and pupils themselves.'

# Learners and teachers

1

# Listening to the learner

**Craig Jones** & **Kevin Smith** | Students, Scotland

1. Space Unlimited
can be found at:
www.elearningscotland.org/
SnippetAccess.aspx?id=88

**Two Glasgow school-leavers, Craig Jones and Kevin Smith, describe their involvement in the Scottish-based project Space Unlimited[1]. The Space Unlimited approach means having the freedom to explore potential, ensuring that ability and curiosity outrank age and status. It was tried out for the first time at a two-day event at the Arches, a vast art space in Glasgow and experienced by around 700 teenagers. It offered them the opportunity to use multimedia, including making a documentary on schooling through the twentieth century, to explore new approaches to learning.**

## How it started

Unlike Kevin I joined after the Arches, so I don't really know what happened there, but basically each school had a Space Unlimited team. We had a big meeting and every school decided what they wanted to do for their project. Shawlands wanted to look at learning through the ages: they made four classrooms – from the 1920s, 1960s, the present day and the year 2040. In my school, a temporary multimedia room was built for three days and we produced a documentary film lasting seven minutes on what the first years of the secondary school thought of e-learning. Notre Dame took a media approach, producing newsletters and magazines and a news report about e-learning. Knightswood School made what they called a Futurerooma about what learning would be like in the future.

## 'Do what you want'

When it all came together, what really struck everyone – although it hadn't really hit us earlier – was that we were in charge of it: we owned this process and the teachers didn't have a say in it. They had an opinion, which we didn't have to accept. It was really exhilarating after 16 years of being told what to do, to be told, 'Do what you want.' It was strange, but we gradually got used to it and found it a very good way of learning. In fact, one of the teachers in my school said we would probably learn more from this project than in some of our classes because we would build so many skills, like confidence, organisation, problem-solving and communication.

We developed an educational timeline to show what education had been like over the last century. A team of pupils, including myself from Shawlands, developed rooms, one from the 1920s, the Sixties, the present day and the future which we created in a museum in Glasgow and then later re-created at the eLearnInternational conference at the EICC. You can imagine the formalities

of a conference and then having a modern-day teacher showing a 1920s clip: it had a magical effect, opening up the delegates' eyes. The 1920s classroom situation scenario was acted out with the times tables being dictated to the pupils, just to give them a taste of what life was like back then.

1.1

At the conference, we wanted to show a teacher telling the delegates what was different, while one of the pupils is thinking, 'No, in fact it's still the same.' Why not ask the pupils what they think would help them most to learn, because they're the ones that are going to learn? Not many pupils of our age have this option; most are conditioned to believe that all the rules laid down are correct. They have been battered with this stuff over the centuries; all these artificial pressures have been put on teenagers. Their views aren't encouraged; instead they are dictated to by teachers who take all the responsibility that shapes their character. Even today, school is not really different from the 1920s. They don't have permission to batter us, but we're still in an institutionalised straightjacket: there's no freedom and that's what we tried to show at the EICC – that we need to change ways of teaching and learning. We have the technology at our fingertips with the Internet – it's just that the way it's being taught is wrong.

We moved on to the Sixties and Seventies, focusing on the music, which we felt to be a kind of foundation for teenagers – something that got them through life, the basis of their learning and what they looked up to. They generally left school at 16 to get a trade, and many were then stuck in dead-end jobs. For the Sixties we didn't want a classroom-type scenario: the teacher was still in charge but you had students standing around practising and doing things. The way we presented this was more like a concert. We wanted to show the real learning that went on. You didn't really pay attention in class, and you still don't. 'When do you pay attention?' we wondered – and it was to the music, which was in your face at that time. The anti-establishment message that was promoted during the Sixties was 'Turn on, tune in and drop out.' I like all those Flower Power messages but most of them have been lost because of classrooms and ways of teaching.

In the case of the present-day classroom, the emphasis was on boredom: we tried to get the message across that this is what the classroom scenario is like: the teacher stands at the front; you sit down. In the afternoon the adults and everyone from the various companies we'd been working with got a taste of how primary children are taught: they all came in and sat down at a round table and found it difficult not to talk. You can't sit at a round table with other people and not talk, and that's what we're going through.

At school today you're told that as a boy you will learn better if you sit next to a girl. I don't know what that's all about (maybe girls work harder than boys?); then the next time you're told it's better to sit in fours so you sit in a round group. Next year it's changed again: you sit in twos, but you don't have to sit next to a girl, and they just keep changing it. Every year I was sitting next to someone different. OK, I made more friends and it might have changed something slightly, but I don't see any point in changing every year if they're not going to stick to a solid format. There's no continuity. They are trying to think of new ways but it's not making any difference and they're going about it the wrong way. They seem to be stuck in this traditional teaching mode, which is disastrous. The reason I'm leaving school is because I'm taught only what they want us to know. I'm sitting in a classroom through no choice of my own and I think if we were given a choice to be there or not to be there, or even if we were given no responsibility whatsoever, then we'd search for responsibility.

### Multitasking: the 2040 classroom

I was speaking to someone at the EICC and we came up with the idea of having an open school for life where you learn what you want to learn for a certain period of time and then leave and it's there, your whole life from beginning to end. We had an interesting discussion about whether it would work and what would go wrong. It was a nice idea and, although I know this sounds like a contradiction, I think if we were able to choose whether we want responsibility it would make all the difference, rather than be forced to do what they want us to do. In the classroom of 2040 we tried to re-create that.

With our budget, we re-created the Space Unlimited Arches Event that we first went to because we thought it was a wonderful learning environment. I know 700 pupils being told to go and do what they want seems a scary concept but as far as I know there was no trouble – no fights, nothing got damaged, graffitid or broken – because they were all given responsibility. Everything was put into their own hands. People misbehave and become destructive in a classroom because they've got nothing better to do with their time. They have no other way of having fun other than winding others up. When that's taken away from them, as it was in the Arches, the effects are astounding. There was a lot more learning done, and in terms of personal and social development, it was a great experience. We tried to re-create as much of that as we could.

When we did the filming we captured the animation on their faces compared with the bored looks. In the usual classroom scenario, the teacher has all the responsibilities, but in our 2040 classroom we introduced the idea of students' multitasking. We wanted to show that children and young adults who have not been able to concentrate on more than one thing are quite capable of doing so. After all, when they go home they'll be listening to music, typing and studying all at the same time. Many of the websites teenagers visit demand attention and concentration – and then there's MSN Instant Messenger, where you can hold conversations with as many people as you want, all at the same time; and this is what we do for leisure, to wind down. In schools, the opposite is the case: we're not expected to be able to do more than one task at a time and we're consequently being spoon-fed individual pieces that make our time spent there boring. Having more going on at the same time is a healthy pressure that we can handle. It's a contradiction in terms for the school to be trying to turn us into responsible adults when we are given very little responsibility, so that whatever small task we are given it isn't enough to keep us on the ball and it's easier for us to slip.

1.1

---

'Children get bored in school because they're given nothing of interest to do, and some teacher, who's intent on having all the power and control, is giving us no other option but to do one thing at a time.'

---

Sometimes you're multitasking and don't realise it. While we were involved in the project and even though it was really serious, there were highs and lows; there were arguments and times when we all got on. Working in teams of 3–7, all the schools met and talked about what they had done, saying this is where we went wrong and where we went right. I'd be talking to Kevin and we would be listening to my team simultaneously. We were writing down our own work, and doing all this at the same time. I didn't realise I was doing it and it was multitasking. If we hadn't done it that way it wouldn't have got done at all. Looking back, I don't know how we did it. I think everyone on the project understands the same thing, even the adults that helped us.

Children get bored in school because they're given nothing of interest to do, and some teacher, who's intent on having all the power and control, is giving us no other option but to do one thing at a time. That might suit some people, but others might want to move at a faster pace. Sometimes in schools I think you're getting shaken when you don't need shaking or vice versa. So it would be good if we were given the option regarding choice.

### E-learning

My school focused on e-learning and multimedia. If you want to learn how to use a camera, or editing or acting or whatever, you have to go beyond secondary school, and go to college or university. So we said, 'Why not do it in school?' The animation we used at the start of our film was drawn, scripted and storyboarded by 11-year-olds. They made up all that about e-learning. We told them, 'This is what you're learning,' because they didn't know. In 15 minutes they came up with a story about computers and jotters being the pupils and the blackboard being the teacher and we asked them, 'Are you for or against e-learning after what we've told you?' We told them about the disadvantages of e-learning and they were still all for it. What they tried to show in that animation was that computers have more advantages than jotters. I know there's more to e-learning than computers, but that was what we wanted to get across: computers were better, more interactive than jotters and you don't fall asleep. One of the youngsters described it as like having 'a delete button instead of a rubber'.

We had 44 pupils make a documentary about e-learning and so we ran a workshop telling them about e-learning. The teachers had nothing to do with it. We – that's me and six other pupils from the school – ran a workshop of 44 'hyper' first years, which – surprisingly – went quite well. Our deputy head came to see what we were doing because we were left on our lonesome running their 44 pupils. He was actually astounded that they were listening to us.

---

'If I told them to do that,' the deputy head said, 'they wouldn't listen to me. How are you doing that?' 'Because we don't shout at them and we ask them to do it nicely.'

'I think I'll go back to training school,' he said, utterly gobsmacked.

---

'If I told them to do that,' the deputy head said, 'they wouldn't listen to me. How are you doing that?' 'Because we don't shout at them and we ask them to do it nicely.' 'I think I'll go back to training school,' he said, utterly gobsmacked. We were impressed. With the first years we'd been too busy saying things like, 'Can you go and sit down please?' and 'We need you to do this,' and they'd do it straight away. There were no questions. They would only ask what they were doing if they got stuck, but there was no 'I'm not doing it.' They just did it and got on with it – which we didn't notice until the deputy head pointed it out.

Maybe they listened to us not only because we were students like them, but because we did it differently to how the teachers did it. We didn't say, 'Do this, do that, do it in five minutes.' Instead we'd say, 'We'd like you to do this and to know what you think about it, so write it down and when you've finished give us a shout.' Obviously we gave them a bit of a time limit on it: you can't just say we're here all day because we did want to get home at some point. But after that they made up five questions about e-learning and what they thought of it, like 'What is e-learning?' 'Is it expensive?' 'What will it do for the future?' 'Can it help people who don't want to learn?' Then during the three days' experience of the temporary multimedia room they answered their own questions in their own ways through a documentary, which wasn't done just by standing up and answering it, in a boring way, but by using different scenes, locations and situations.

The film lasted about seven minutes. In one scene we showed that sometimes teachers go too fast and children sometimes learn by a hands-on experience rather than by listening to a teacher going 'Blah blah blah, is that fine, have you got it right?' So it turned out that the pupils knew it better than the teacher because they'd learnt it interactively rather than sitting writing it in a book. They looked bored when they were just listening and they wanted to show that e-learning is a lot more interesting. One of the scenes that stuck out for me was the 'joyrider' scene. The scene showed a youth driving a car, not interested in learning, and then discovering that e-learning made it more interesting for him. It showed that everyone could learn from e-learning.

1.1

The joyrider was quite funny because he's a great little actor. He is autistic and attends the communication disorder unit in the school and we wanted to include this, because this unit want to learn as well and they understood the concept of e-learning. It was great how even with a disorder they knew exactly what we wanted and what they wanted – communication was on a high. All the pupils in the film were 11 or 12 and came up with every scene and every answer. People don't give enough credit to the first years and don't listen to them as much, and for them to come up with that was just astounding. We showed it to the whole school last week. Everyone loved it and thought it was great: they couldn't imagine how 44 first years could come up with something like that. We pulled some strings to get into Rangers Football Stadium as well, so they were quite happy with that.

We got them to show all of the countries to demonstrate how e-learning can be used anywhere in the world, not just in Britain. We put a huge green screen behind them, adding in the background later. That's how we did the car scene as well. But the kids were really up for it. They loved the whole idea of multimedia and said, 'This is great, we've never done this before, it's really fun.' We had an evaluation afterwards and every pupil wanted it as a subject so they could learn how to do it, because although we only ran it for a few days – we filmed it, made the music, and edited it in three days – they all wanted to learn how to do it. They couldn't really do everything, but they had their influence in everything and they would tell us, 'We don't like that scene', 'We like this scene' and 'We like that bit of music.'

They got hands-on experience but they wanted to do more and that's what really encouraged us to make that room a permanent room, which is what we're aiming towards. We've got a room sited in the school and hopefully it will become permanent. They were really keen on e-learning, even though they understood it was going to be expensive, because computers aren't cheap nowadays – no wonder Bill Gates gets £770 per second every day – it's unreal. So we were really taken aback by what the first years were saying. Hopefully this room will become permanent because right next door the BBC is moving into a huge complex.

### The open school

In an open school where you can learn what you want, there can obviously be a big divide between what the teachers think we need and want and what we think we need and want. But I believe you first have to look at what the kids want: to become an electrician or an RAF pilot? Obviously not every kid in the school knows what they want to become, and there's where you've got to give them the range of the curricula so that they can have a wider choice.

Our generation has been brought up on computers. I think some of the students would like to have a program developed to monitor them through their schooling from primary through to secondary like a guidance teacher or an electronic report card, which is fun, personalised and appeals to the user. This could be approached whenever they wanted to and would give out useful advice from an onboard data file or the Internet. I think this program, in order to be successful would have to be as near to artificial intelligence as we could get.

---

'If the boundaries are subtle and not in-your-face there's less chance of people wanting to rebel against them.'

---

You need foundations, perhaps at primary school, so that in the very first year you can make the right choices for yourself. Then you can have the option to go either to an open school, for people who don't feel the need for as much structure as they get in a modern school, or a traditional school, for those who feel they need that structure. How an open school can keep some sort of order must be to do with boundaries. At my school there are too many boundaries set. The instincts of a teenager are that the second they are forced to do something, they rebel against it. The rules are too in-your-face, so the way we handled those 44 first-years was by not setting too many boundaries for them. Rather than saying, 'These are the rules and you must follow them or you'll get a punishment exercise,' I think if the boundaries are subtle and not in-your-face then there's less chance of people wanting to rebel against them and trying to disrupt the learning.

If you go to college you usually work half the day so you have time off. The teachers aren't then going to say, 'If you don't come to your class I'm going to send a letter home to your mother.' They expect you to come to college. It's an unspoken rule: you go to college because you want to learn. But you're forced to go to school and I really don't see them changing that rule because everyone needs an education to get a job. But what we're saying about the open school is that if there are fewer rules you'll find children will adapt to them a little easier and that's why college is a perfect example for a high school.

I don't think there will be time when we use our PCs and Internet at home rather than going to college or school. We are teenagers: we dress up to impress other people, we love socialising (or the majority do). We need the social interaction as well. Technology is good but a balance is important and perhaps certain aspects can be done from home on a PC – this is already happening when a teacher might say, 'Finish that folio in the house' and we go and type it up – but we still need to see, hear and feel first-hand in order to learn as well.

### Teaching the teachers

One of the biggest problems is getting teachers to adopt new learning approaches. At my school, when pupils choose what Standard Grades or GCSEs they want to study, all that is compulsory is Maths and English, a couple of periods of PE every week and a period of RE. So subjects like Modern Languages and Sciences don't have to be selected at all. It was mostly the older teachers who didn't want to change. To educate the educators is really difficult: you can't teach an old dog new tricks. Even though you're trying to teach the learners you've also got to educate the teachers. Their career may span 30 years, but they've got to adapt to the times, otherwise classrooms become boring.

1.1

Teachers have to move with the times and in Scotland teachers go away on courses and are taught how to use computers. Glasgow has an initiative where every school's networked: I can go to Kevin's school and log on as my name and get all my files and I can go to any secondary school in Glasgow and do that. But the teachers didn't know how to do it, so they had to be taught how. To promote this the Government said you'll get so much money if your teacher comes and learns how to do that as well as other computer skills. (Unfortunately the money had to go on the school and not on trips to the tailors!)

To educate the educators they run courses and I think that's the best way: it shut teachers up and it worked. You have to take that chance. If it doesn't work your senior management team is going to look stupid, but I really can't think of a way round that, that's not really my job. Just as children learn in an open school so teachers can learn in an open environment because they want to learn. But it's got to come from above, from the Government. It will take a lot more than one or two schools adopting an open learning approach to make any fundamental change.

Everybody's got to complain about school; everyone in a school will have an idea how to run it better. But that's a promising thought – not that everybody's got a complaint, but that everybody's open for a change. So if you had to give the school a blank sheet of paper and say let's start again, there would be many changes. If we gave older teachers these new tricks, they'd be more susceptible to change because they'd been given the choice of what they'd like to have in the school rather than what we would like to have in the school, because in order for everything to function, we all need to be happy. If they are learning with us as well it might have a better sense of community. Maybe if they're not seen as teachers but as mentors or facilitators, even friends, rather than authority figures you just don't like – I mean nobody really likes anyone in authority – we'd have a different attitude to them. If you're opening the school up to the pupils, open it up to the teachers as well to express their opinions. If you're going to listen to pupils you have to listen to teachers, they work there, they don't want to come to work annoyed with work every day because they'll just end up saying 'early retirement at 45' and that's it.

## What the Government should do

If the Government listened to our ideas on this subject and did something about it, schools would begin changing over the years. I couldn't say it would be definitely like this or like that, because things always change. As I said before, the example of whom you sit next to may affect your education. The people who come up with these theories won't just stop. They will continue to change things, falsifying one theory and trying to prove the next. And the Government will also listen to them. In the future though I hope the fundamental values that we talk about today are in place – that teachers will become mentors/facilitators. That's when decisions are made; everyone involved who has an opinion is allowed to express that opinion – pupils and teachers. Recognise that not everyone learns in the same way. Everyone should be motivated by others to do better than yesterday – teachers and pupils. People shouldn't be underestimated and should have the space to go with something and be wrong, and not be afraid.

1.1

# Learners creating the learning environment

**Shirley Alexander** | Professor of Learning Technologies,
University of Technology, Sydney, Australia

**Shirley Alexander discusses a school-based research project that allows children to set the agenda in deciding what e-learning they want in school, thus creating more potential for sustainable learning.**

### Students as designers of e-learning: an ARC project

I'm involved in two Australian Research Council (ARC) funded projects involving schools with children ranging from year 2 (aged 7) to year 11 (aged 16), so there's quite a variety of ages across both projects. One is a longitudinal study looking at whole school communities and how they use ICT in teaching and learning, which has been running for three years. The other project (led by Associate Professor Lynette Schaverien) involves working with students as designers of e-learning, such that the students decide what they want to understand and then design the environment in which they develop their understanding. The multimedia development team from my group – the Institute for Interactive Media and Learning (IML) – built the environment which the students designed. A part of the research project involves investigating whether the long-term sustainability of e-learning environments is greater using this approach than the traditional process (which is rather patronising) where we, as experts in e-learning, design e-learning environments for the students to use. In the latter case, neither the design nor content is really the students' own, even though they might provide feedback about projects developed by others as members of focus groups.

Over the course of this project, I've been stunned and greatly impressed by the ways in which these students think about the world, about the questions to which they think they know the answers, and the kinds of questions they say they still have. Looking at those questions, and the ways in which they propose to answer them, I have realised that they're incredibly good researchers at a very young age.

The approach we took was that in each class the students came up with a series of questions and then the whole class determined which of those questions they would pursue. Some of the initial questions included, 'Why don't we eat our fingernails?' and 'Is space really empty?' Eventually, the three schools involved narrowed the list down to two questions: 'Why do we think and how do we think?' and 'How come we're not born knowing what we know now?' Then in groups, back in their classes, the students had to determine the ways in which they might explore the answers to those questions, and record what they did and what they found. They did this in

curriculum time rather than in their own time. This was not the usual approach to curriculum or teaching for their teachers. Nerida McCredie, the PhD student on the project who made many valuable contributions, developed detailed Investigation and Design kits to support teachers as their students investigated their questions in classrooms.

The plan was that they would have two lessons per week in each class to participate in this. The kits anticipated, for teachers' benefit, the kinds of questions children might ask as they investigated: was this a good way to find out the answer to that question? Why or why not? How could it have been better? Is there something we can use for the design of our e-learning environment and if so, what? How might we use this in our design? How can we record these ideas for the design team? And so on. And then we asked the children to develop mock-ups of the ideas that they had about how the computing environment might look. The students were encouraged to sketch these out on a piece of paper or submit them as design documents. Two representatives of each of the 12 classes across the three schools brought these mock-ups to a two-day meeting here at UTS [University of Technology, Sydney] where they presented their schools' ideas, and my development team listened to their ideas and started to frame up a design brief, all the time trying to be true to what the students had decided they wanted to do. Then we came up with a formal design brief, just as we would for any other client in terms of what the project might look like, as well as a development timeline and an initial costing.

1.2

### Content development

Once our development team costed their design, we discussed the fact that it would cost about half a million dollars, and since we only had about one-tenth of that, the students had to do what real clients do and pare it back. This involved lengthy discussions about what they thought were the major features they really wanted, and what they could leave out. This process went back and forth, until we came up with a project scope that was achievable within the funding limitations. We've just finished the (almost) final version of the project and the students have had an opportunity to review it. One of them said, 'Oh yes, this is exactly how I imagined it would be.' They've done amazing things in terms of developing the content for the project. They have asked serious questions and have gathered what information they could find about them from books and the Internet; they have designed and carried out experiments to try and answer the questions, and they have videotaped interviews with a range of people who have different views on how we think and why we're not born knowing what we know now.

---

## 'One student said that a learning journey would be one in which you don't know the answers until you yourself have thought about it.'

---

At one of the primary schools, for example, they interviewed a psychologist and a psychiatrist about these questions, and at the end of that process these professionals commented that they felt they'd been put through their paces and had had to think very hard about their responses.

They decided that the project should be presented as a journey where the user encounters various objects which can help in answering the two questions. There was a lot of discussion about whether it should be a railway or a forest, and they eventually decided on a forest. But I want to emphasise that it was the students themselves who designed this project, and I remember during one of the design discussions, that a student kept bringing the others back to thinking about how the user would make sense of each of the objects (pieces of evidence) in terms of bringing it all together – how would they answer the fundamental questions they had originally posed. Marlene Scardamalia, the developer of CSILE[1] (Computer Supported Intentional Learning) who developed the Knowledge Forum, talks about how we tend to trivialise what we do with kids: we use the idea that they have to learn the basics first which they then build on. She talks about a different approach where kids are confronted upfront with the fact that these questions and answers are quite complex. So they start off with the notion of complexity rather than trying to build on the notion of simplicity, which has real implications about how we teach, and what it is that we're teaching.

1. Details about CSILE and the Knowledge Forum ca be found at http://ikit.org/

In terms of what the students have designed, it differs significantly from content designed by adults for children. They're incredibly sophisticated in their thinking about the experiments and links they've designed. One of the outcomes of the discussions around the persistent students' question: 'But how will people answer the question for themselves?' was that they decided to have a notebook. While it might sound like standard practice to us to have an electronic notebook, they were really interested in how people might use it and the kinds of features the notebook needed to have in order for them to use it. They've been far more sophisticated than I had ever imagined they'd be when I first got involved in the project.

One student was saying that you shouldn't be told the answer about the journey. He said that a learning journey would be one in which you don't know the answers until you yourself have thought about it, but that might not be the answer, it's just what you think at the time. The students liked the idea of contributing their own responses to the questions which could be available for others to look at as part of the learning journey. In that way they thought that users could learn from each other, not just from the other resources on the site. Their reasoning was that if the user thought there was just one right answer, he or she could go and use the environment to learn about other possible answers and then they might actually think, 'There's a good suggestion, that's better than what I thought,' so they're learning through the journey. These are all quite interesting ideas about what learning actually means. We tend to try and help people see what the 'right' answer is, but these students already know that there is no right answer; it's just the way that one thinks about things and how one uses evidence to back it up and justify it. That's what's really fascinating to me.

These students have grown up in the digital era where they're used to being able to videotape interviews and do little animations and drawings. If we'd asked the students to design a learning experience without using computers, I'm not sure it would have been as imaginative if they didn't have the technology to use as a tool. In fact they may well have been frustrated by the fact they didn't have those tools. For this environment they have used video, animation, sound and obviously the Internet is an important part of that.

1.2

It was a personal journey for them but it's also a collaboration: there is an ideas board so they can look at other people's ideas and comment on them.

| Brain Damage | Chatterbox | Children Play | Distractions | DNA |
| Drawing Tests | Dreams | Evolution of Language | Factors Affect Learning | Jacob the Rat |
| Media | Obstacle Course | Recall & Recognition | Senses | Ideas, Questions, Challenges |
| Sheep's brain | Stress | Toy choices | Twins | |

GENESIS  ► NOTEPAD  ► MAP  ► EXIT  ► GLOSSARY  ► HEL

Students' e-learning design

As far as bringing in different aspects of the curriculum rather than having separate subjects is concerned, it seems to vary from school to school. Of the three schools involved, one particular school has been so convinced by the value of this approach that they want to do a lot more in that way. In terms of implications for the future classroom, I think we grossly underestimate what kids are capable of doing, the questions they're capable of generating and the ways in which they are capable of thinking through different approaches to understanding the topics. We hear about schools where students sit in class and write down what the teacher says or copy notes out and so on. There are much more imaginative ways to involve them right from the beginning about thinking about what they need to learn, how they might learn it, what counts as evidence, how they weigh up different pieces of evidence and how they build their own arguments for what they think. This kind of approach has a lot of promise for school education in my view.

The difficulty lies in how teachers are going to cope with this new approach. I've been quite horrified at seeing what some teachers actually do, how they can actually stifle students' creativity and trivialise the questions they ask without even realising they are doing so. The students are capable of so much more than we give them credit for. So the outcomes of this project should have a huge impact on teacher training. In particular, the way that we do a lot of technology teacher training is to teach them how to use spreadsheets or databases or develop multimedia themselves, but that's the worst possible use of their time. What they need to be learning is about using exactly the kind of process that the project uses, which really is about learning and understanding more about how to make use of the students' learning approach such that they do ask questions and try to solve them themselves. What we should be doing is helping teachers learn what tools might help the students to solve the questions themselves and how to be a good guide and mentor, rather than how to be up at the front of the classroom telling students the facts.

Students' e-learning design

### Effecting change

Change is an incredibly difficult thing to effect, especially in organisations such as schools. People have been teaching and learning in traditional ways for so long that these approaches to teaching have almost become part of what we learn in school. To change these views is a major cultural shift. People such as Seymour Papert have been saying for some time that we have to break schools before we can fix them, and I hope we don't have to do that. However, the idea of incremental change, which is what we've been trying to do over the past ten years, just doesn't seem to be working fast enough to achieve what we really need to achieve. There are some interesting pockets of innovation, but those innovations are not being diffused as rapidly as they should be. I don't know what governments can do about that. They can legislate all they like, but unless they can win the hearts and minds of the teachers, they're not going to change anything.

Perhaps it's about presenting evidence and putting in place the systems actually needed to support these kinds of learning experiences. This involves changing curriculum, changing assessment and changing teacher training. These are all parts of a big system where each of these components interacts to result in change or not. The schools are our partners in this, and we'll be presenting all of this evidence to policy-makers.

---

'If you have the students involved in doing the design and leading the development of projects, then is it more sustainable than those projects that have just been imposed?'

1.2

---

In the other project that I'm involved in, a longitudinal study of schools' computer use, we've found that, despite all the rhetoric that comes out of computer companies and governments, there is very little evidence of large-scale change in schools. Although there's a lot of use of ICT, it's nowhere near as sophisticated as much of the rhetoric would suggest. I was really excited a couple of years ago when I saw the Jason Project,[2] which is an online expedition where students are the researchers. There were examples of whole schools adopting it. There was even a school in Australia that changed its whole science curriculum around to base it on the Jason Project. But examples like that are few and far between. By and large ICT is used as a reward or as a kind of 'bolt on' activity, rather than being really integrated into learning.

2. Details of the Jason Project can be found at http://www.jasonproject.org/

Although these schools are all wired and have Internet access, they're not really making good use of it. There's a whole complex system of reasons why not, including the fact that there are a lot of teachers who just don't feel competent to make good use of ICT in teaching. Some feel that everybody else knows what they're doing and they don't, and by and large the teachers don't get adequate time release to go and experiment with the technology. It's a real dilemma for me, because on the one hand there's this project which is actually quite depressing, and on the other there is this other really exciting project where the students have designed and overseen the development of a wonderful e-learning environment, and where the process of doing that has been even more important than the eventual product. Most of the funding (AUS$50,000) has gone into the design of the features and building the tools around it, and the students have supplied not only most of the content, but also the design vision.

3. Coburn, C.E. (2003) Rethinking Scale: Moving Beyond Numbers to Deep and Lasting Change. Educational Researcher 32(6), 3–12.

A part of the e-learning design project is to try and look at the degree to which this kind of project can be scaled up. Cynthia Coburn recently wrote an article in *Educational Researcher*[3] where she talked about different ways of thinking about what it means to scale up. There's the kind of replication of the project in other schools and there's the adaptation of the project to the particular context in other schools. These schools have to take on the ideas behind the project but use them in another way so that they have an impact on the quality of teaching and learning outside of the original project. Then there's the whole idea of sustainability. Can this project be sustainable over a period of time? That of course is what our research question is: that if you have the students involved in doing the design and leading the development of projects, then is it more sustainable than those projects that have just been imposed? Of course, it will now be interesting to see in what ways these approaches might become embedded in participant schools as the first next stage of a much broader research agenda. We need to see if, by gaining greater equity in e-learning development for the students themselves, e-learning in schools might be able to scale up more successfully.

It's just a question of how we're going to turn that into other subject areas and how we can actually bring it together and have the variety that keeps students motivated. How sustainable is this if they were doing this all day every day – would they get tired of it? I think variety is really important; but what we really have to think about is whether we should be working by imposition: telling them what they have to learn and how they're going to do it, rather than letting them come up with their own big questions: what do they find easy to understand, what do they find difficult to understand, and changing around the curriculum to take account of that? Obviously there are basic things we need to integrate such as mathematics and arithmetic, and reading and writing, but there's no reason why it has to be taught outside the context of learning to read something or learning the mathematics or arithmetic around solving a problem of interest to the student. I think it makes it much more interesting for the students to be doing that. Now that we have so many technological tools available, what makes a big difference is that speaking is now on an equal footing with writing because we can digitally record it, and we can include videos and so on.

Some of the students are incredibly excited about this project. I have been out to schools when these students (who have been representing their school on the project) have been asked to report back to a whole school assembly. I happened to be present one day when one little girl in particular got up to speak to the whole school and she had her speech all prepared on little cards. She held them in the palm of her hand and was reading from them, but at the end she said, 'And it's nearly going to be ready and I just can't wait.' She was so excited and I thought about what a great privilege it has been to work on this project.

Contact details for the project team

| | |
|---|---|
| A/Professor Lynette Schaverien | UTS: Education |
| | Lynette.Schaverien@uts.edu.au |
| Professor Shirley Alexander | UTS: IML |
| | Shirley.Alexander@uts.edu.au |
| Ms Nerida McCredie | UTS doctoral student |
| | Nerida.McCredie@uts.edu.au |
| Dr Robin Hall | UTS Researcher |
| | Robin.Hall@uts.edu.au |
| Project information site: | http://www.iml.uts.edu.au/genesis |

# Schools in the community

**Marian Brooks** | Executive Director, Cambridge Education, England
**Eddie Brady** | Principal, Unity City Academy, England

**Marian Brooks, Executive Director, Cambridge Education and Eddie Brady, Principal of Unity City Academy, review their experiences of introducing radical ICT-based strategies into schools where they were principals.**

## Teaching in a multicultural setting

The area of west London where I [Marian Brooks] was head teacher is culturally diverse, with traditionally blue-collar workers around the airport and a burgeoning degree of industry. Virtually all industry around the area is related to the airport, either through direct labour or associated service industries. There were waves of Kenyan and Ugandan Asian immigrants, many of them graduates and well-established economic entrepreneurs, who took up blue-collar occupations with considerable aspirations for their youngsters, but real ambivalence between their cultural sets and what their children might be exposed to in terms of the British national culture. Historically, there has been a lot of racial tension, some between the immigrant populations and whites but, increasingly, as immigration diversifies, between populations themselves.

There were 1,400 students in the school but every week we would admit students in every year group, most of whom had little or no English and some from appalling backgrounds. Unfortunately it is assumed that if someone is a refugee and now settled here everything is absolutely fine; nothing is really done to address the trauma the children and their families have been through. We did a lot of monitoring, particularly when value-added tables and league tables became significant; they became meaningless when the raw statistics showed that 50 per cent of those who started in year 7 (age 11) were still there in year 11 (age 16).

## Application of ICT

We were using ICT very heavily. The focus was on tracking them: with that sort of mobility their records, which are always paper-based and scanty to say the least, are very difficult to locate. Social services and liaison across different authorities are a nightmare. The notion of grouping children by age rapidly went out of the window. Tracking the students in this scenario meant we had to amend most of the MIS systems we had running in UK schools. These were geared towards age grouping and needed to be adjusted to allow us to track by different criteria.

We also needed to be able to teach highly individualistic curricula. A student might be completely lacking in English and not able to access parts of the

curriculum, so very often we wouldn't try to teach them geography or history etc but would focus on something they could do, such as additional French or maths, and we'd give them extra language support. Everybody who came in had a buddy teacher, a mentor – not necessarily their form tutor, who tracked them on a very tight, regular basis.

We developed highly visual ICT-based induction packs. We showed students pictures and with the aid of additional language fonts we made the induction packs available in most major community languages so that students had something they could learn from. Importantly, though, the real issue for us was to involve parents in that process. Parents arriving as refugees are desperate to get their children into school, but the alienation of adults from secondary education is even more marked than the language barrier, since they are not familiar with the culture. So, we did a lot of work with local community groups and faith groups to draw parents into the school, and offered everything from familiarisation to English language courses to basic ICT, to cookery and dressmaking. We gave facilities for all the community groups to meet without any cost so that the school became part of the community. This meant the community were not only contacted when there were problems: we went to the community because it was a resource and welcomed them in.

1.3

We based social workers and a housing officer in the school so there could be a one-stop shop where they could help avoid the confusion of trying to sort out all the logistics of being in a new country. By being in the same place and joining that up through talking to social services and housing, it was much simpler and gave the students a much better chance. The ICT was developed to sit in the middle of the processes and the intranet was always totally open with parents encouraged to use it. There was a surprisingly high level of computer home ownership, partly because parents felt that home access was something they could provide, but the school was also open from 7.00 am until 10.30 pm as a community resource.

### Extended School policy

In 2000 we prepared a paper for the Department for Education and Skills (DfES) focusing on methods and costing and this has formed the basis of the current Extended School policy. At that point we were getting 3,500 adult users a year; there were parents' drop-in sessions after school, the learning resource centre was open continually until 8.00 pm for anybody to use and we never charged for Internet access; we were fully staffed so that parents could come and talk. There were always teachers there. It didn't matter who came, they would have access to somebody to talk through a problem and be made to feel both more secure and that the school was accessible.

---

'One of our goals was to involve parents in adult education so that their children might see this as an exemplar they would wish to follow.'

---

This had a huge impact on the children's learning and commitment to school. All the evidence is that family involvement is vital, so I was seeking overt not just tacit family involvement. Another goal was related to the modelling of learning behaviours; if children see parents reading or learning at home they're more likely to read and learn. So one of our goals was to involve parents in adult education so that their children might see this as an exemplar they would wish to follow. As a result our staying on rate post-16 was 85 per cent, which is much higher than both the local and national average. Of those who stayed on, we had over 80 per cent going into higher education, which was remarkable given the low competency profile of so many of the students.

The policy regarding classroom access to ICT was that this had to be anywhere, anytime. ICT wasn't a separate area, it embedded everything. Teachers couldn't work at Cranford unless they were IT-inclined. It had to be seen as an enrichment, as a tool that broke down a lot of the barriers over language access. Motivation was the other huge driver I had to make me equip the school with ICT. These students saw themselves as less worthy. They were on the receiving end of a considerable amount of racism, so we went for high-quality environments. They had to believe that they were fantastic because look at what was being put in front of them. So we went for saturation ICT, for the highest quality. They would never have to say 'Where can I go and find a computer?' The computers were there. Eventually we had one computer for every two pupils, and every teacher had their own wireless laptop. In the classroom we had desktops, laptops, palmtops – our definition of access to ICT was anything that works.

### Funding

It was funded, frankly, by educational prostitution. I wrote bids for every scrap of funding available. We had some huge boosts, such as big National Lottery funding and specialist school status in my first year there. We obtained ongoing sponsorship from companies with whom we developed real productive collaborative relationships so it wasn't a one-off. We took the view that we needed to be seen as good neighbours and give something back to the companies and, in some cases, address some of the corporate social responsibility agenda which was then emerging. There was certainly a strong shift towards looking for long term employment prospects but a lot of the time it was to do with experience for their own young people. These companies often wanted to give their young graduates leadership experience, so, they would come to us directly as part of their training. We assisted British Airways considerably in developing their staff languages programme and diversifying it into community languages, and set up outreach programmes for the company in its overseas settings, particularly in South Africa and the Middle East because of our connections there. We did a lot of work building websites for the British Airports Authority and we did all its planning for safe routes to school around Hounslow, with the students directly involved in all these projects.

### Advancing students' learning agenda

There was no point in doing any of this unless it advanced the students' learning agenda. So there were two aspects. One was the business and industrial application side; the other the internationalism embedded into a statement of entitlement: that every child should have a curriculum enriched by experience of the real world and enhancing broader understanding of the UK and its place in the international family. Next to that was a very personal agenda about combating racism and valuing the experience that all these young people brought from all over the world, and that what they brought to the school was a richness rather than a problem.

1.3

This extra-curricular experience was planned into each Key Stage of subject areas and unless it fitted in and enhanced what we were doing, it didn't happen. But what it did do was replace a lot of the arid, abstract approaches to learning. The other thing that we worked very hard at was involving adults other than teachers in the curriculum. It was much easier to do this by virtual linkages, by ICT, than by bringing somebody in for a one-off visit. We used both phone and video. We first used an ISDN system donated by Brunel University, but it progressed very significantly and really made a difference when we started using webcams. Although it was very low-key, we did a lot of minority languages teaching by video distribution, particularly as I couldn't afford a full-time teacher and we had a couple of available students who could help out. That worked very well, but the real breakthrough was on webcams and collaboration, which has moved on considerably.

We wouldn't go out to look for teachers with technical skills but for people whose view of learning was really about pedagogy, who understood the active involvement and the different ways children learnt. With that comes an inevitable openness – an attitude of 'why not?' If a teacher said 'Why should I use ICT?' then he or she was not suitable. Our teachers have to be willing to take risks, so we deliberately appointed risk-takers and highly creative people who were secure about their own persona and standing, and weren't looking for traditional relationships that reinforced models of seniority with the teacher being in control. We wanted people willing to let go and allow a bit of creative chaos. Occasionally we got it wrong and we'd appoint somebody who found it very difficult but we'd rapidly come to an agreement that this wasn't the right place for them.

The students were expected to be totally responsible for their own learning. They needed to know what was going on. They had open access to all their assessments, they sat and worked on where to focus, where to put the effort in, what to do to get it right and, therefore, it had to be an active engagement in a relationship – not a question of 'You will do this because I say so', with the children expecting to be told why they were doing something and what they needed to do to do well at it.

### Building and networking

The building undoubtedly has an enormous impact on how readily we were able to individualise teaching. If I could go back to Cranford and start again I would go further with a blend of open, diverse, well-equipped learning spaces so that students could access and recap and revise, use video, use any resource possible to revisit learning. I would go for much more flexibility. It really needs a blend of large classrooms coupled with an increase in smaller spaces, to ensure that we can achieve a more intimate environment, somewhere that could be set up so that students could have long periods of time undisturbed. I would probably look for a rooming model that has about a 30 per cent bonus on it, recognising that if it's not being used by students, adults need to be there during the daytime.

We built an enormous amount of staff working area and networked it with staff's own working spaces, which is absolutely vital. Staff need somewhere that is their place to be able to go and work and access their resources and facilities, but the staff rest area was also the community lounge where they mixed with adults and the community and was a grown-up place. Post-16s and those older age groups need the same thing as well. So if we make a point that all adults in the community work in the same way then we're really making a big difference.

---

'It's about saying, how do schools serve the community, how do we connect to the people we serve?'

---

### Connecting to those we serve

The students had free time. My own daughter is fast-tracking on a couple of subjects in a very traditional school and I was told, 'Next year she'll have to do some more subjects to fill her time,' so I asked, 'Why can't she just study individually on the rest of her commitments?' and was told, 'No, she's got to be in the classroom.' They couldn't see the point that the environment, ethos and culture in a school should be set up so that the focus is on what students need to do in learning. There are clear patterns of behaviour where, if students aren't treated as if they are herded cattle, they'll behave in a normal way, and they need adults who aren't necessarily scrutinising them but who are there as a support. Students need free time to catch up, focus and determine their own pace of work.

We had a lot of students in all age groups who, because of the demands, didn't come in all the time, who worked from home and they would all have individual timetables. If a student has a major problem with dyslexia (we also operated the dyslexia unit for the borough), and have no English to speak of, then I'm not going to put them in areas where they are guaranteed to fail. I'm going to focus on things we really can do.

A lot of our recovery programmes were ICT-based. It didn't make a great deal of difference whether a student spends time reviewing video material or using an individualised study programme, and they could do that from home, then why not do it from home because they also happen to be the oldest child in a family and their mother's got diabetes and is in a bad state? So don't make social problems with the families by saying they have to be here from half past eight till half past three. Work out a way that works for families. As they got older, a lot of our students were prime breadwinners in the family and if I'd said 'No, you've got to be in school', they would have left school. We may not be able to get them to school during the daytime, so we'd put them into the adult education classes in the evening. They could work for the majority of the day or do a morning shift and then come to school for the afternoon and the twilight session. It's about saying: how do schools serve the community, how do we connect to the people we serve, rather than saying you, as a student, have to conform.

1.3

## Doing things differently

While working for a high school in Northumberland at the start of the 90s where I [Eddie Brady] was deputy head I started thinking about how we could do things differently around learning. My thinking around this had begun ten years earlier but it was not until I went to Northumberland that I found the environment to begin to move this thinking forward. My thoughts were around how the delivery, engagement and access to learning all might be improved. I was also beginning to explore my interest with technology and how we could develop the technology to do that. I had this idea that high school could actually be the host for the curriculum material and a technological base and platform for all the schools in the area. We could get into the streaming of applications to the various schools within the town. So my thinking started around the technology. Although the technology wasn't available to make it happen, or at least so I was told, we had started on that path. My view was that using the technology we could set up virtual learning spaces – at the time I called them clouds and these could be accessed from anywhere and at any time. I also believed that learning should be around the stuff we do in school but it should and could be around health, social development and interaction or community-based learning. It could be about anything that people would be able to access. The technology could also be the tool for finding out.

'We were creating a learning culture not just about what was happening in school, but what was happening around the school and community and further afield.'

## Hermitage School, Chester-Le-Street

In 1995 I went to Hermitage School in Chester-Le-Street and began developing some of these ideas. The technology was now becoming available. One of the things we wanted to use it for was to deliver learning directly to business. We also wanted all our students to have individualised learning programmes facilitated by an adult who happened to be a teacher and we wanted to put technology at the heart of this. We began to use the technology, to develop a culture around learning and technology, using it for the development of higher order skills. This meant realising that the process involves technology right from the start. You actually think with the technology in front of you, as opposed to when I first went there and people were just typing up work they had already written. The biggest moves forward in the technology were when we achieved specialist school status, based on technology and when the school won the National Lottery. As the first school in the county to achieve specialist status, the funding allowed rapid investment. With the lottery win the majority of the staff went out and bought computers. Staff having computers at home or their own laptops started to make a real difference.

When I first went to Hermitage, staff weren't used to the technology and did not have access to it. Once we started to bring technology in we used to find ways to create imperatives for its use. For example, one of the first things we did was to provide a template for the school development plan on disk: at the lowest level, people would actually have to put that disk in the machine and at least print it off. It was just to get people to start using the technology. Because we now had the technology, people started to enrol on programmes to develop skills, which was really positive. A huge community focus was developing around what we were doing and we were creating a learning culture not just about what was happening in school, but what was happening around the school and community and further afield. Then we really started to develop the right culture around learning. Young people saw adults learning both in the evening and during the day. Often these adults were the parents of our students; they were setting the tone, the example, helping to establish the culture. Drop-in facilities were established with refreshments available. We began to run programmes for local business and we became a Cisco Networking Academy for both adults and our own full-time students. We were open all day and each evening, every week of the year. Students came to use the technology in the evening, before school in the morning, and during the school holidays.

1.3

When I arrived at Hermitage, it had 700 students, with less then 50 at post-16. The school opened at nine, closed at four and also at lunchtime. There were no part-time learners, exam results were 32 per cent, numbers were falling and morale was low. When I left, exam results were 57 per cent, best ever, it had over 1,000 students full time, with over 150 in the sixth form and 2,000 part-time learners on a weekly basis; it was open 51 weeks of the year. Students were in at 7.30 in the morning learning and were still there learning at five, six at night; they were going in over holiday time to use the facilities to work on their assignments. It was a really thriving learning community.

### Unity City Academy (UCA), Middlesbrough

I had been wondering what I was going to do for a couple of years; there was so much scope at Hermitage, I could just stay there and push things on. We'd started developing ICT in the school and we were being seen as a national leader in that whole area. So I wanted to see how these ideas, contexts and principles could be applied in a really challenging place. I thought about going to a very difficult part of the country and seeing if the sort of things we'd been thinking about and doing could actually work. So that's how I got to Unity City Academy (UCA), Middlesbrough. I didn't think it was going to be as difficult as it's proving to be. I thought that everybody was ready for it, but that hasn't proved to be the case. We've got to do everything we can to make a success of it and we're slowly making a difference. There is a growing culture around learning, a certain confidence around the students; we're creating a new freshness among staff. It's a long road, but there are lots of really positive things going on.

Unity is a City Academy and City Academies are about trying to make a difference in really challenging parts of the country. A lot of thinking was taken from what was happening around the world as well as from the Department for Education and Skills' own thinking. City Academies' aims are about raising achievement. UCA is about new models of delivery, particularly using the technology; new ways of working with young people in the communities; focusing on vocational aspects based on the remit with which the academies started.

### Taking responsibility

We don't have to adhere to the National Curriculum and we have considerable flexibility. Although there are some good things about the latter, the focus is not really about the National Curriculum, but about how learning is delivered; how young people engage in learning and getting them to take responsibility and ownership in a supported way.

The way we're getting students to take this responsibility is first of all telling them that at the end of the day they are responsible for their learning and their outcomes as well as those of their peers. While we're there to support and help, the responsibility lies firmly with them. When we have conversations with young people, we're talking about their work and how they're progressing and no matter what the issues happen to be, whether it's about behaviour or how they present themselves, it's really about how that's affecting their work. We are also offering access to the facilities, so we're trying to break down this idea that learning takes place between nine and four, or whenever school happens to be formally open. If a student wants to come in at eight in the morning or still be here at half past five, these facilities are available. Nine times out of ten there will be somebody there to help them do that.

The other way is to begin talking about and developing ideas about individualised learning programmes. Students are beginning to see that it isn't about a group of 25 or 30 children, it's about the students as individuals and how they each progress through their learning. We have to have those same conversations with staff, because if we can't convince them that this is the way to go then they won't be able to do it with the students. One of the biggest barriers is getting the staff on board for some of those ideas.

'The focus really is about how a student learns, how learning takes place and the processes they each go through.'

### Contextualisation and relevance

One of the issues around learning is that it always needs to be contextualised if it is to become relevant. We're looking at Key Stages as a learning space: with all the years of study within a Key Stage forming one learning space in which the aim is for particular objectives and outcomes over that period of time. We need to look at where we are starting from and build on that. The second thing is relevance: let's say we are facilitating in history and talking about revolutions, then we'll start by looking at Middlesbrough, the way the students are and the revolutions that have shaped the landscape in Middlesbrough – how the Industrial Revolution shaped Middlesbrough's industry and how the Technology Revolution destroyed its industry. Then we look at revolutions in other parts of the country, in Europe, even Iraq, So we contextualise it from where students can understand it and build and move out with it. We're making it relevant to them and presenting it in a way that they can engage with as opposed to expecting students sitting in east Middlesbrough to understand what's relevant about the French Revolution when it's an important event in history but beyond students' reach because it's not contextualised.

1.3

Within each learning stage, students have destinations to reach. I've talked about 'revolutions', that's an example of one of their destinations – but there might be others, such as Ormesby Road (the road the school is on) as a soap opera, or about a magazine or magic. So if Ormesby Road is the basis for the soap opera, that's the destination and the students build on what previous students have done, so the soap opera continues. Whereas if the destination is something like 'magic', then that might form the basis for something that's happening around science such as experiments. Every time a student has completed a destination they get a stamp on their passport, so they're collecting these destinations as they go through the Key Stage, but they're also collecting assessments around their learning and collecting significant destinations on the journey of their learning within that Key Stage.

### Learn to learn

The closest we've got to starting on this is to develop our 'Learn to Learn' programme, currently operating in Years 7 and 8, which we're going to revamp for September along some of the same lines. The idea is to move away from programme-based learning and take an almost thematic approach to learning, underpinning it with the basis of the City Academy programme – the thinking skills, collaborative skills, and process-based learning. The focus really is about how a student learns, how learning takes place and the processes they each go through. The content then becomes a vehicle for developing learning. We argue that the challenge is to build capacity in young people to become expert learners. We're not going to do that by hammering content into them. What we've got to be looking at is the processes, skills and competences we need; it's about learner capability. It's not the content that's crucial, it's the process.

Technology enables us to start individualised learning, where students not only take responsibility in terms of what they're doing, but in assessing where they are in their learning. Some of the assessment tools around technology are around limitations: it's not just assessing how many times a student picks the right answer, but where they are in terms of their thinking around the process they're undertaking. We're also looking at setting up learning in a series of web pages so that students may go to particular pages to guide them through their learning. As they're web-based they won't just rely on students being in school, they can access the resources from anywhere and still continue their learning at home. It's also about finding bits of learning appropriate for students and creating the mechanism to bring them together so teachers can begin to create individual programmes, individual courses for students. If, for example, students work through a particular piece of learning and come up against something requiring skills using, say, Word, then there's a guide, a signpost to take their learning somewhere else which then allows them to come back to it with new knowledge or understanding and move on. The technology also allows students to work together, either on site or offsite. They can work individually or in a group and use the technology to collaborate.

> 'Students should be building a portfolio
> of assessments demonstrating what they can
> do at the level at which they can do them.'

We're still an exams-based country and schools at certain times of the year start to become exam factories. We need to move away from that kind of assessment and be accrediting much more widely significant learning. We have students who spend their time processing information on spreadsheets or other applications, and we then ask them to sit down for a couple of hours and write. We need to think about how we use the technology for assessment and move away from these summative assessments. Students should be building a portfolio of assessments demonstrating what they can do at the level at which they can do them. The assessment should take place when they're ready to be assessed, rather than at the end of Year 9, 11, 12 or 13. We should develop a culture that says, all you're doing with your learning when you're assessing it is checking what your foundations are. The foundations allow students to build on the next piece of learning and strengthen those foundations as they go through. We need to establish a greater value, a wider range of learning and assessment, and move away from seeing exams as the only thing that gives us an indication of where students are. In other words we need much more assessment for learning.

### Building and networking

The academy is about to move to a new building. We'll be open for business in September. The building creates different kinds of spaces for students and staff to learn, depending on the types of learning they're involved in or the people they're working with. The technology will be deployed around breakout spaces and learning resource centres, but there will also be mobile technology and wireless connectivity for laptops etc, or groups of people within classrooms who will be able to use that technology. If we're working in maths and want a group of students to be working interactively, say with Maths Alive,[1] then there's the facility to do that. On the other hand, if students are working on a particular piece of mathematical learning and need to use Maths Alive, we can send them to breakout spaces to log on, access and get on with that piece of learning.

1. Maths Alive makes use of interactive whiteboards and specialist software to engage and motivate pupils in mathematics learning – see http://www.rm.com

The other thing about the technology is making it available over an extended period of time, whether it's 7.30 in the morning or 6.00 at night. One of the difficulties with the area we live in is that only 20 per cent of students have technology available at home, so many students would be at a disadvantage and creating opportunity for access is a priority. If they can't access it at home, they need a place where they can come to access it. Students who do have technology at home will be able to dial a freephone number and be connected to the academy's facilities at little or no cost. We have to work out what the barriers to access are and break them down, and this also applies to staff. We're installing a 100Mbs link into and out of the academy, so in terms of access, that's never going to be a problem for us for the foreseeable future. At the moment people pay for broadband so we need to think about ways of breaking down that cost barrier. Similarly with the issues around low home penetration, we are a Cisco Networking Academy and from September 2004 will be offering the IT Essentials Programmes as a way to begin to solve that problem. Our intention, at least for the first cohort of students, is to allow them to keep the machine they build. Whether we can do this for subsequent students we will need to see, but it would be a great way of increasing the access at home. Not only that, we also intend to increase the entrepreneurial spirit in this way. Possibly we can use our students to offer advice to others in a small consultancy organisation. Perhaps our students with their knowledge will work in the local computer shop, who knows?

1.3

### Community involvement

We're already starting to involve the community. We're developing a full service school model and community learning is going on both on-site and off-site. As with all community initiatives, it's always easy to attract people who are keen to learn, but the biggest challenge is attracting those who until now haven't seen learning as a valuable activity in which to be involved, and then the chances are their sons and daughters won't see learning as a valuable activity. Currently there's probably little or no support for learning at home, so school becomes a place children just have to go to, by law. That's part of the culture change we've got to make so they see learning as a valuable activity that makes a difference in their life and economic circumstances. We won't get 'personal or social regeneration' unless we get economic regeneration, because regeneration is all about benefits. If people see that learning has economic benefits, then they'll want to be engaged in it. Over the next ten years there will be huge development around Middlesbrough's infrastructure. There will be more small businesses, retail outlets and technological businesses and we must ensure that our students – Middlesbrough people – are taking those jobs as opposed to people coming in from elsewhere. We want to keep the best talent in Middlesbrough.

In ten years' time the academy may no longer be seen as a school but as a community enterprise resource at which people are registered. Some of the learning programme may take place at Unity, some may take place at home or in other parts of the town, possibly with other providers. But Unity still has a responsibility for learning, particularly for young people. I expect to see a lot more online learning. There will be even greater responsibility for learners themselves to be in charge of their learning and a huge community involvement in what we're doing. Learning may or may not be delivered by a teacher, depending on the type of learning. It might be delivered by someone from a local company: if we're working on a module in marketing, then the marketing director from a local company might come in to deliver that module. So we will have real engagement and real responsibilities for the learning of the people in Middlesbrough. It's not just the school remit but the community remit. The community becomes that learning resource.

The qualities we're looking for in members of staff are the same ones that we're trying to develop in young people. During a staff learning session I was working with a group and I was describing where we were moving to in terms of the transitional curriculum, to transform the local neighbourhood into a learning community, with everybody being a learner and taking responsibility for their learning and access to that learning based on the growth dynamic. I was describing the skills I expect of members of staff who operate in such an arena. They are the thinking skills – people knowing how to learn, being creative around their thinking, being good decision-makers, systems thinking, problem-solving, being able to reason, work with diversity, showing leadership, able to negotiate around learning, making sure you're serving the needs of others but at the same time having integrity and self-esteem, taking responsibility, being a team worker as well as being able to work on their own, facilitating the learning of other people and yet a good self-manager in terms of their own learning, and of course having the necessary ICT skills. That's what a principal needs from their staff if they are going to do the things they want to do and believe in.

1.3

# New skills for teachers

**Manfred Wolf** | Central Institute for Teacher Training
and Staff Development, Bavaria, Germany

**Manfred Wolf, of the Central Institute for Teacher Training and Staff Development, discusses the development and progress of the 'net@schools' in the state of Bavaria, Germany, to train teachers in greater understanding of school networks and trouble shooting problems.**

S et in the former theological university of Dillingen, founded in the Middle Ages, the Central Institute for Teacher Training and Staff Development (Akademie für Lehrerfortbildung und Personalführung) was established in 1971. The Institute provides a range of support services to all Bavarian teachers for all phases of education and subject areas and is responsible for planning, teacher training, organisation and moderation. We offer teacher training for different levels, at regional, local and school levels as well as within the academy. We also provide other services for all four levels and evaluate the success of teacher training.

The Institute is responsible to the Bavarian state through the Bavarian Ministry of Education and collaborates with ISB, a central institution in Munich which is, for example, responsible for learning objectives, lesson plans and curriculum. What makes the Institute special is that we're one of the largest Cisco Networking Academies in Germany. We have an excellent relationship with Cisco, having started the Academy programme in 1999. We were delighted that, through this programme, we had the opportunity to improve the quality of vocational education in the field of IT. We have about 40 vocational institutions, mainly technical schools providing three years' training in IT in Bavaria.

The Cisco Networking Academy program was one of the first ever approaches to blended learning. After conducting substantial research on e-learning approaches, we investigated the Cisco Networking Academy program and were surprised at its quality. There were already proven best practices in the US so we were glad to become involved and began training the trainers who would teach the Academy program in technical schools. To date we have trained 100 trainers, all of whom are vocational school teachers working in technical schools. These trainers have qualified as Cisco Certified Academy Instructors (CCAI) and are working in 40 local Cisco Networking Academies teaching about 4000 students. We have a staff of five in the Institute in Dillingen supporting these local academies.

### Dillingen's overall objectives

What is particularly special about Dillingen is how we have developed the concept of 'net@ schools' from the Cisco Networking Academy program. The concept is to provide a service not only to vocational school teachers but also to teachers from other types of schools, especially system operators. These system operators are teachers – they're not from industry – who are in charge of maintaining school networks and whose smooth running is critical in ensuring that schools make good use of technology. The network plays a key role in providing access to modern, attractive content that is motivating and multimedia-based. If schools want to introduce multimedia they must have a network structure and network services. However, the system operators currently working in schools have little or no knowledge of networks, even though most of the problems or challenges are based on the smooth running of these networks. The idea behind net@schools, therefore, is to use the competency developed in vocational schools to disseminate knowledge and build up more competences for staff working with the network in primary schools, secondary schools, Gymnasien, and Realschulen.

1.4

The Ministry reacted very positively to this initiative as they are well aware of the challenges we've been describing. It has always been an issue that system operators are unable to offer their colleagues the services they demand. They in turn have problems finding the support they need to help them troubleshoot problems, and so the Ministry was very keen to find a solution to support system operators because of their key function inside schools.

A key element is to empower people to bring their best to the community and help them with their technical services. There is a German expression meaning 'explaining things strengthens people'; in this context it means you have to solve the technical problems but you also have to support people by providing high-quality training. If people recognise that what we're providing is helpful, then they'll accept it and be more motivated, which is exactly what net@school is designed to do.

### Network infrastructure

This course is related to the Cisco Networking Academy curriculum, which in turn is strongly related to the network infrastructure in schools and the use of a school network structured in a different way and for a different purpose than, say, a factory where there may be more data but fewer programmes. It was important to devise a training programme that focused on school logistics and related issues and problems. This meant that the Cisco Networking Academy program curriculum was not specific enough for school network administrators and contained more technical information than was necessary for this audience.

For example, in a primary school there might be a central printer connected to the network. If that printer doesn't work, those using the network might assume the printer is switched off. Few will understand that the printer has an IP address that is either not on that network or hasn't been configured correctly. System administrators need to know basic things about troubleshooting, such as whether the LED blinks green; whether there's a layer 1 or layer 2 connection; pinging to test the layer 3 connection; or whether IP connectivity is there, before phoning a local firm to tell them that the printer isn't working. The normal procedure would be not to make any of these checks but to make a phone call to the external support service to say the printer isn't working and nobody knows why. Our aim is to help the system administrators to give that qualified failure message or error message.

It isn't just a question of giving better services to local teachers, but also about ensuring maximum efficiency – saving time and money – by understanding the system. If you're thinking of total cost of ownership, it doesn't make sense just to bring high-technology devices into schools without building up competences to use that technology, otherwise it becomes very expensive. Schools end up having to pay for maintenance and a lot of phone calls. However the biggest problem is that people get upset because they want to use the technology but it doesn't work. Many system operators say they have to work long hours and don't get paid overtime, but they waste time because they're not qualified. If they had simple troubleshooting skills, they would save time and phone calls and would be much happier, and this is just what we're aiming for.

The net@school project is structured in several stages. We have a 'double multiplying' system because we want to reach 5,400 system operators in a year. So, we need a snowball effect which is a double-step multiplying system. We have a network of senior trainers, trainers and system administrators. The senior trainers are part of the 100 vocational school teachers trained here on the Cisco Networking Academy program. These senior trainers are running local academies so they already have the infrastructure in their schools. They also have the Cisco Networking Academy labs, which they use for training the trainers, which has helped immensely in implementing the net@school programme.

The trainers gain their qualification in local academies and then come to Dillingen to learn about the equipment they will use for their own teaching or training. That's the second step. We have developed a network cube for training which is a flexible mobile cube where all assets and active networking devices and equipment are integrated. We have cabling, plugs, switches, hubs and routers and we use the network cube to demonstrate typical installations

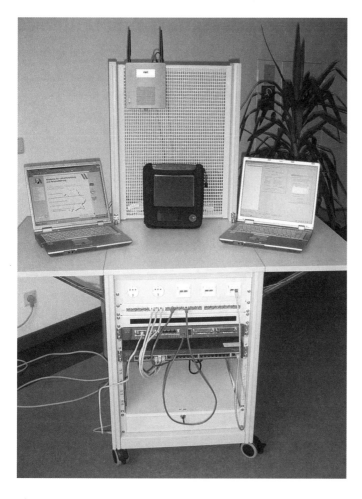

Figure 1

of school networks. We don't want loose installations, which can be the root of many network problems. In fact 60–80 per cent of errors or failures in schools are caused by these. We want to show the correct installation through the network cube: we can prove the installation is working and check it through measuring devices. We establish protocols and demonstrate the strength of the signals.

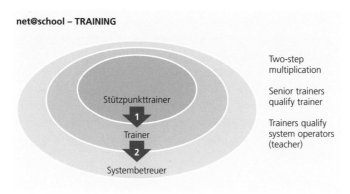

**net@school – TRAINING**

Stützpunkttrainer

1

Trainer

2

Systembetreuer

Two-step multiplication

Senior trainers qualify trainer

Trainers qualify system operators (teacher)

> 'What we have learned can be summed up by
> the idea that you have to be challenging to be able
> to support and you have to challenge yourself.'

These network cubes are important because we want to place emphasis on practical experience. E-learning is very important but it's only about a third of the training – two-thirds comprises practical work. So out of 60 hours' training, 40 hours constitute practical work and 20 hours e-learning. We use the network cube as the basic infrastructure for training system operators.

**net@school TRAINING FOR TEACHERS**

| Start | Preparation | Lab | Support |
|---|---|---|---|
| 1 Introduction Concept Material Organisation | 2 E-learning Self study Tests Collaboration | 3 Hands-on net@school Labs Skills test | 4 Help desk School net applications Teamwork |
| 1 day | 4 weeks | 40 hours | 3 months |

## Joining a net@school programme

All Bavarian schools have been informed by the Ministry that the net@school programme is a suggested solution for information gaps and knowledge deficits. Local teachers will have a chance to apply to take part in local training from September 2004. We have built up 96 training regions in line with Bavaria's 73 counties and 23 cities, which are local authorities for developing school infrastructures. In each county and city area we organise group training for 12 system operators. We will have 180 trainers from these regions who will ensure that local teachers get relevant training related to their individual needs.

## Challenges

Looking after a school network can be difficult for local teachers trained to teach, say, physics, English, German or mathematics. It can be an additional burden for them, especially when they are teaching full-time yet their principal has given them the additional responsibility of the school network. Discussions are currently in progress about whether teachers should be responsible for the school network rather than a specialist firm or the city or county. Meanwhile, we believe our school network programme is meeting the deficits and demands. Additionally, because there are relatively few companies who can be financed to service schools' network maintenance and there are often no competent firms in remoter areas and because of the typical school logistics there needs to be some degree of competency and knowledge in schools provided by teachers.

We need to bring it to the point where we can qualify teachers as system operators to create the right environment for teaching and learning. Our net@school qualification should help to maintain a school network and certainly provide the necessary skills to give qualified error messages for second-level support. If we're proficient we can resolve the problem of teachers' conflict between their two roles. The conflict is there and we have found a way to respond to it.

### Lessons learned

We are now in the middle of the project and have received feedback from the schools. In the pilot phase, we have been through all the levels I described: senior training, trainer training, system operator training at the local level here in the county of Dillingen, and we've had a very positive reaction.

What we have learned can be summed up by the idea that you have to be challenging to be able to support and you have to challenge yourself. Teachers are recognising that it's real help, and practical support for the real world. Even though it's not yet happening on a wide scale the pilot results tell us we can be confident of developing net@school successfully across Bavaria.

1.4

### The future for net@school

We've tried to introduce the basics of networking for local system operators but we shouldn't stop there. We should also build up further modules, such as how to use the networking operating system for networking services in schools. There is the challenge of a server–client environment which is related, for example, to an active directory structure where there is a need to define classrooms, students in the classroom and teaching services. So, these networking services need to be taught as well.

We've had extensive discussions about what our starting point should be. The decision was made to start with layer 1, 2 and 3. Now we have to move up to the application layer 7. We have learnt to think and work in seven OSI layers, especially when troubleshooting a network issue. Therefore we want to expand net@school with modules 2 and 3. Module 2 will be for Windows networking operating systems and module 3 will be for UNIX, and especially Linux, operating systems, related to school needs.

I have two final comments on our teaching which can be summarised by two German expressions: 'Dinge erklären, Menschen stärken' ('explaining things strengthens people') and, from the perspective of the participants, 'Die Hilfe zur Selbsthilfe ist die grösste Hilfe' ('The best kind of help is helping someone help themselves').

# Teachers and the Internet

**Dmitry Guzhelya** I Director of the Federation of Internet Education, Russia

**On its fourth anniversary, Dmitry Guzhelya reviews the success of the Russian Federation of Internet Education's Generation.ru project, a pioneering teacher training ICT programme.**

### The Generation.ru project

In April 2004 the Federation of Internet Education celebrated four years of implementing our Generation.ru project in more than 40 Russian regions. Generation.ru, an innovative educational project, was developed in 1999-2000 by the YUKOS oil company. Originally, it was managed by YUKOS, but soon the team was joined by others, mostly educational practitioners. For their work, the Federation's creative team was awarded the 2002 Russian President's prize for education.

When we started we thought we were just developing a project to meet the common goals set by the YUKOS management. These goals were set in clear terms: Russia's role in, and influence upon, the world community must not be based exclusively on its natural resources. A competitive Russia is, first of all, a state using and developing advanced technologies, and, most important, creating them. To build a civilised society, to participate as a peer in the civilised global community, Russia needs to make its information available to the rest of the world and to provide equal access to information domestically. An up-to-date, hi-tech Russia will be built by a new generation of its citizens, mainly those who are still school students today. We need to begin instilling an information culture in them immediately so that they become used to searching for, analysing, using and creating information.

It was clear enough that our objectives required schoolteachers to be involved. Teachers can and should represent the information culture and instil it in those we call the new generation. But teachers need help, new knowledge and skills; they need to learn how to use IT in their work. This is how the core idea of Generation.ru was born: to train teachers in Internet technologies.

The project originators realised that they had to take into account Russian educational reality. At that time, general education was only beginning to recover from crisis, and IT was regarded as alien to real life. This was understandable when teachers were not being paid their salaries, schools had extremely poor materials available, and many other serious problems persisted.

The developers expected society initially to distrust a non-profit-making project from a major private company regarded as 'oligarchical'. We knew that some would regard it as a mask of decency to cover selfish ends and also that YUKOS alone could not solve all the problems of introducing IT into education: it would have been irresponsible to claim that it could do so. As a result, the following decisions were made that substantially determined the dynamic character and success of Generation.ru:

- While not attempting to solve the entire IT problem, the project should give a strong impulse to the introduction of IT into education and become an organic part of a process which, we were certain, would move forward rapidly in the near future.

- The educational system, teaching community and society in general need to be clear about the project and its goals, objectives and results.

- When implementing the project, effective means and methods should be used, providing immediate high-quality results and establishing stable patterns of functioning and development.

We came to an important conclusion that was to contribute significantly to the project's success: while being non-profit-making, the project should not be a charity. We needed multilateral partnership with authorities at all levels, the public and other representatives of the business community outside YUKOS.

The project's goal was to help bring IT to general education. The key objective was to organise free training for schoolteachers in most Russian regions on how to use Internet technologies in their daily professional activities. We determined the results we wanted to achieve in the next few years: by 2006, we expect to have created 50 regional Internet Education Centres; by 2007, training should have been organised for at least 250,000 Russian teachers.

### Educational programmes of the Federation of Internet Education

By September 2000, the Federation had already developed a number of educational programmes and educational methodologies (more than 15 altogether) and had them certified by the Ministry of Education of the Russian Federation. With time, we acquired some experience and came to the conclusion that the programmes required unification in terms of professional orientation, training time and the initial level of our students' knowledge and

1.5

skills. We created a modular system of programmes and methods, 'Internet Technologies for Education', which successfully passed a state inspection and was recommended by the Russian Federation's Ministry of Education as a tutorial for use in the professional development system.

Speaking of our educational programmes, an important point should be emphasised. Initially, no one raised the question of what kind of teachers we dealt with: everyone assumed that our project was for teachers of computing. We explained that all teachers, regardless of the subjects they teach, need to know about IT. Today it goes without saying; but back in 2000, it was not that obvious.

### How regional centres of the Federation are established

Educational programmes and schemes are important and necessary, but our project required much more. Apart from knowing what to teach, we also needed to figure out how and where it should be taught. We needed an infrastructure to train teachers in Internet technologies. We have already mentioned that Generation.ru provides for the establishment of a chain of Regional Centres of Internet Education, which has always been one of the key objectives for the Federation. Our specialists developed a technology to create and maintain such regional centres: inside the company, we call it the conveyor. It is based on standard requirements imposed on the centres' technical configuration, their structure, staff, establishment schedule and so on.

A typical Regional Centre of Internet Education has four computer classrooms able to house 40 students. Each computer in the centre has a high-speed (128 Kb) Internet connection. There are multimedia projectors, screens, printers, scanners and digital video cameras in every classroom. Since training is continuous (six days a week) and each programme takes 80 hours to complete, each centre has an annual throughput of more than 1,000 graduates.

The Centres of Internet Education are established as departments of the leading regional higher educational institutions, universities and institutes of professional development for educational specialists. This approach helps accelerate the process of establishing the centres. The results achieved prove how effective it is: there were 7 centres in 2000; 19 in 2001; 31 in 2002; and 41 by the end of 2003. Very soon, the number of graduates will exceed 100,000.

### Partnership between authorities, the public and business

Each centre is a joint project of the regional administration, a university providing a base for the centre, and the Federation of Internet Education. Along with organisational resources, which are certainly important, funding is handled jointly as well. When a centre is established, the region provides a building or part of a building to house it free of charge, decorates it at its own expense in compliance with Federation standards, and pays for the Internet connection.

In turn, we provide equipment and furniture, organise all work, and finally deliver the centre as a turnkey operation.

Funding for the regional centres' operation is also provided jointly by the regions and the Federation. The regional administration pays for transport, board and lodging for students arriving from other towns. The Federation pays for everything else to do with the organisation and running of the educational process in the centre (the salaries of tutors and other staff, the cost of maintenance and so on).

Regional educational authorities play a very active part in the centres' operation. They include ministries, committees and Departments of Education – the names of the authorities varying from one region to another. Their key task is to organise groups of students, which is an important and difficult task. When they are spending time training with us, teachers temporarily leave their own jobs, so they need to be substituted for, and that's why accurate advance planning is vital.

We have created an effective model of partnership to ensure that Generation.ru develops dynamically: apart from being innovative and educational, our project is also cooperative.

1.5

## How regional centres of the Federation operate

We are doing our best to make the atmosphere in our centres as comfortable as possible for students from the very first day of their training. Reasons for discomfort can include the novelty of the subject studied, the unusual training style, or the long-time habit of teaching instead of learning. We took this into account when designing both the centres and their activities.

Each centre is designed to make the students' group and individual activities effective. Students from other towns board in the same building or nearby. All the rooms for each centre are located close to each other, interior decoration is in light colours, and equipment and furniture are light in appearance, too. We believe strongly that the colour of equipment and furniture is important.

On the first day of training, we ask our students to fill in a questionnaire. Based on results, we form groups of ten students whose knowledge of computers and the Internet is roughly at the same level. Our tutors are key specialists from higher education institutions. To join our team, they have to pass a competition organised by a commission made up of representatives of the regional educational authority, the university that provides the basis for the regional centre, and the centre itself. Regardless of how long a tutor has been working with us, after the first training session we ask each group of students to fill in another questionnaire. This enables us to find out whether information is being delivered comprehensibly and conveniently.

Now that we have gained some experience, we can say that in every centre our students' uneasiness during the two weeks of their training decreases in a more or less similar way. The uneasiness is at its height in the middle (or sometimes by the end) of the first week. The turning point is the middle of the second week, at which point students become absorbed in the training. By the end of the two weeks, most graduates say they wish it could last longer.

Each student, regardless of their original knowledge and skills, is expected to develop a graduation project during the period of training. This must be an educational Internet resource (such as a personal home page, a website for their school, or an online lesson for more advanced students). Projects are presented to fellow students, instead of to a panel of experts. The presentation of certificates always ends with a little celebration of everybody's own and others' achievements.

### Students and graduates

When launching Generation.ru, we were concerned about who our students would be. Statistics say that a substantial proportion of teachers in Russia are of advanced age. Of course, any age-based restrictions have always been out of the question, but training only older teachers also seemed wrong somehow. Our concerns proved to be groundless, although they were certainly understandable, since at the time we didn't know our future students as well as we do now.

Our experience shows that, while the proportion of males to females among graduates of the Federation (80 per cent are female) matches the statistics on teachers in Russia, the average age of those attending our training sessions is below the national average for teachers: 78 per cent of our graduates are below 45.

We have always paid special attention to the training of administrators engaged in education: regional educational authorities' staff, and directors and deputy directors of schools. Managers have real administrative power in general education, and their attitudes determine to a substantial degree the success of Generation.ru and the introduction of IT into Russian education as a whole. In 2000, our Federation developed a special 40-hour Internet technologies training module for administrators of educational institutions. In each region covered by the Federation, we first train headmasters, and then teachers, for whom an 80-hour programme is envisaged. The proportion of headmasters and other school managers amounts to some 20 per cent of the whole student body.

### Attitude to Generation.ru

As Generation.ru is being implemented, a certain distrust by the public is rapidly being replaced by a positive attitude. An important factor is the support demonstrated in public by the Russian government, especially the Ministry of Education of the Russian Federation. The project has quickly begun to develop throughout Russia, allowing specific results to be made visible to all.

The project's launch almost coincided with the launching of Federal programmes bringing IT to education. In 2000, implementation began of the rural schools computerisation programme suggested by V.V. Putin, President of the Russian Federation; and in 2002, a programme supplying computer equipment to urban and rural schools was implemented. As a result of these Federal programmes alone, the number of students per computer was reduced from 500 at the end of 2000 to 145 at the beginning of 2003.

## 'A certain distrust by the public is rapidly being replaced by a positive attitude.'

Mass media coverage of IT in education in general and of Generation.ru in particular also played an important role in forming a positive attitude towards the activities of the Federation of Internet Education. We have contributed to this by providing free access to information about our project to the public. The first specific efforts of our Government aimed at the introduction of IT (computerisation, development of telecommunications and the creation of educational e-content) made the activities of the Federation substantially more topical.

1.5

### Other projects

As well as rolling out Generation.ru, our Federation, in cooperation with the Ministry of Education of the Russian Federation, is also implementing other large-scale educational projects – for example, creating and deploying a chain of regional e-learning centres. Their objectives are very similar to those of the Centres of Internet Education: they prepare teachers to teach Internet technologies in the regions. However, their structure and degree of integration in regional educational institutions differ from those of Generation.ru centres.

Each regional centre has created a chain of small resource centres in the region (in towns and rural areas) and delegates most of the consultancy and educational functions to them. Establishment of such centres allows our students to keep working while attending professional development training.

Other advantages of a distributed professional development system are as follows:

• There is better control over the acquisition and use by teachers of their new knowledge and skills. This is achieved because of constant feedback provided to tutors by students at regional resource centres, and because of the time intervals between training sessions, during which students can use their new skills in practice.

• There is mass professional development at the regional level because of the large number of regional resource centres available. On the basis of the two years of operation of regional e-learning centres/regional resource centres thus far, the throughput of such a structure is 2.5 to 4 times higher than that of a single regional centre.

- There have been substantial savings in local budgets allocated to teachers' professional development per teacher. The Federation of Internet Education estimates that, depending on the type of the region, cost reduction can vary from 2.4 times for compact regions to 4.3 times for regions with a widely distributed infrastructure.

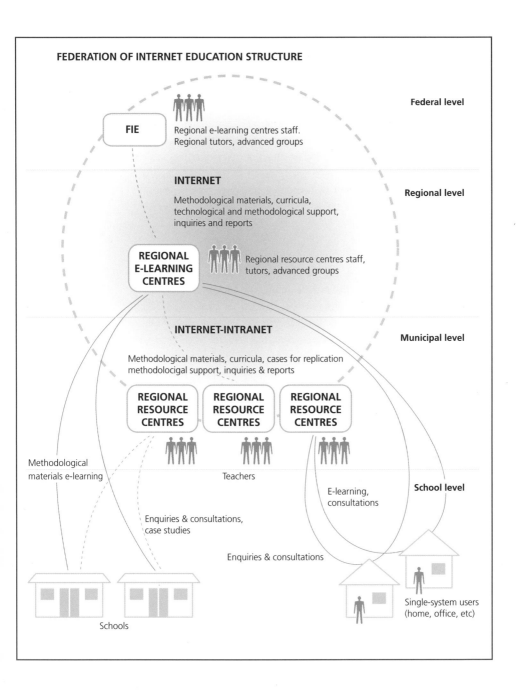

**FEDERATION OF INTERNET EDUCATION STRUCTURE**

Federal level

FIE — Regional e-learning centres staff. Regional tutors, advanced groups

**INTERNET**
Methodological materials, curricula, technological and methodological support, inquiries and reports

Regional level

**REGIONAL E-LEARNING CENTRES** — Regional resource centres staff, tutors, advanced groups

**INTERNET-INTRANET**

Municipal level

Methodological materials, curricula, cases for replication methodolocigal support, inquiries & reports

**REGIONAL RESOURCE CENTRES** **REGIONAL RESOURCE CENTRES** **REGIONAL RESOURCE CENTRES**

Methodological materials e-learning

Teachers

E-learning, consultations

School level

Enquiries & consultations, case studies

Enquiries & consultations

Schools

Single-system users (home, office, etc)

## Some conclusions

Our experience shows that training teachers in new technologies motivates individual and/or group initiative aimed at the creation of conditions for the use of such technologies in practice. Many graduates of our Federation, when they return to their schools, have begun to persuade their managers and municipal authorities to provide more computer equipment to schools and to connect them to the Internet.

Training in Internet technologies is an important factor in teachers' professional socialisation. This is particularly topical for Russian regions and towns with a well developed or developing use of the Internet in everyday life. For reasons beyond teachers' control, students sometimes know much more than their teachers about computers and the Internet. Training in our Centres of Internet Education allows teachers to become at least as advanced as their students in their use of the Internet.

The part of the Generation.ru project that has already been implemented is a prototype of a public system of professional development in the field of IT for teachers. Authorities, the public and business are equal partners within this system. And business here means more than just the YUKOS oil company. YUKOS is the general and leading sponsor of the project, but is not the only one. Financial support is provided to Generation.ru by the Tyumen Oil Company, the Magnitogorsk Iron and Steel Works Open Joint Stock Company, KROK, and a number of other businesses.

1.5

Reviewing results of the four years of operation of the Federation of Internet Education, we realise perfectly well that they are only interim, and that much still needs to be done. The fifth year of work for the benefit of Russian education lies ahead.

# Practical frameworks

# Melting the classroom walls

**Mark Edwards** | Superintendent of Schools, Enrico County, Virginia, US

**Mark Edwards, explains why Enrico County has become recognised globally as a leader in one-to-one computing with its laptop initiative, creating opportunities for connectivity and for students and teachers to learn from each other.**

Learners still need to go to school. But the fringes of school are among the great devices for civilisation in bringing communities together and having common goals, standards and values, being able to work within that framework and understand each other and live together, and that experience of learning together is as much a part of the process as the actual individual learning that takes place. We're living in an era where choice has become very important, yet there is still a compelling force within us to communicate and understand each other. The principles of democracy contain a concept of the common good and common understanding, of being able to work and learn and grow together. Even though some choose the home school route, there's a growing body of evidence that the relevance and importance of time spent together, working together and learning together is a significant factor even for home-schooled students, and in most cases they will still attend public or private universities in a setting where they truly are ultimately going to that place called school.

School is for children, but also for communities and families. It provides the foundation for individuals to better themselves and make choices about their life and function. We're seeing an evolution of the place called school, and of how learning takes place, an integration of both the science and art of teaching. Through the years of analysis, research, best practices and effective learning and teaching, we have developed our capability to provide personalised and individualised differentiated approaches for learning. We're also realising the inherent value of children learning together. The idea that only one individual can convey information is diminishing as we understand the value of regional, national and global communication, and how students are expected to interact as they move into the world of work or of their communities.

We're on the cusp of seeing the utilisation of science and technology in the classroom catapult learning to a whole different level. We use terms such as being able to melt the walls and expand the horizon, and there's an interactivity and connectedness from classroom to classroom and school to school, region to region, even nation to nation, that previously would have been impossible, but with the advent of technology is providing those opportunities.

At the same time it creates a discovery environment where students and teachers may construct new knowledge from a wide array of resources.

In the past three years in Enrico County we've seen an explosion of energy based upon the connectedness that students are finding with a huge venue of resources available online and through electronic technology. It's changed a whole sense of expectation from a route process and with a singular source of knowledge being the teacher, to this anticipation of discovery.

2.1

### Content creation

There are a multitude of sources driving content. The whole venue and era of accountability has created a foundation of state, local and national standards that are integrated into and driving curriculum to some extent, and at the same time, because of the evolution of technology making sources available to students in many places at all times, it has changed the level of curriculum availability. Students are now able to access real time developing information rather than static closed information as a curriculum, and teachers are able to look not just at a single book or source, but provide a variety of avenues for students to understand concepts, explore different aspects of curriculum and really change from a singular look to a very broad look. We're seeing an element of student interest and discovery in learning driving the very best of what we would hope curriculum to be, which is meaningful and relevant information. Moving to digital content and utilisation technology as a primary tool in the classroom has created a specialised curriculum: a single student can explore at a level above and beyond what would have been possible before. So we're seeing more specialised, individualised, personal and relevant curriculum interest. Students are driving it, but it's really the very best of what we've always hoped for in education, which is that students realise its importance – they're energised by it and really want to go on that journey.

In terms of content I see elements of both student and teacher creation. They have a different tool set to connect to and organise information and then share it with teaching colleagues and student colleagues. On a parallel track, dozens of educational publishing houses as well as new digital educational publishers are converging on this space to provide new, broader, more creative curriculum, designed differently, though maintaining basic tenets of standard curriculum. The single biggest difference is the constant link to discovery. Whether it's that actual digital link that you hook onto to go to another space, there's this sense that there will always be another link for deeper discovery based upon the intent of the teacher, individual student or particular class. And that creates a whole different portal for discovery every day by any student, teacher or class.

There are multiple tracks to be followed in preparing students for digital exploration. Students must make choices for themselves about what's right and wrong, and we work with parents and community members to help students understand that life is about choices. In previous years it might have been a choice about looking at a hard copy of something inappropriate or making a right or wrong choice about using somebody else's notes, but they were still choices that had to be made and are still relevant to today's world. Another track is searching for and finding the very best filtering processes and agents available. We've been able to develop within a framework an array of choices for parents based upon individual need and their individual perceptions about comfort levels related to security and to material that might be objectionable. Another key strategy in responding to community need is to provide a level of comfort in terms of filtering choices, looking not just at a singular but multiple efforts. Ultimately, it's an education process: just as there are preparations to go on a journey, the same preparations have to be made for the individual student, for communities and families; there must be a sense of communal awareness of what's important. The very best filter we know of is the parent. If parents are actively involved in that process and monitor, teaching and learn with their children, that can transfer to the student's independent decision.

'The opportunity to share knowledge and information from all around the world really has created a whole new sense of what school is about.'

One of the elements we're excited about in increasing parent involvement is providing opportunities for parents to have digital access and have a different type of communication linkage with teachers through computers and the Internet. Parents are very receptive to using this relatively new communication tool. Through recent software programs we've developed, we've actually increased parental involvement and awareness by providing weekly grade reports for parents rather than nine- or six-week grade reports. Parents have immediate ongoing access, through which they also have opportunities to communicate online with teachers. This has created a sense of timely information and togetherness, and even though processes must be taught, learnt and developed through that, parents and teachers agree that this has enhanced the quality and timeliness of communication. Rather than waiting for a report card and seeing a disappointing grade – a D or an F – when parents are provided with formative information not driven by an enquiry but ongoing in terms of dissemination, they can intercede before there's an issue or become involved in supporting or helping. It saves time for teachers who have an assurance that parents have accessed this information that sometimes might get lost on that pathway from school to home when left to be delivered solely by the student.

## One-to-one computing

Enrico has become recognised globally for being a leader in one-to-one computing with our laptop initiative. This has created a sense of opportunity for connectivity and for students to learn from each other, for teachers to learn from each other and create a greater sense of community, whether it's the local community from school to school, or the greater regional community from city to city, or country to country. That part of the whole concept is changing students' aspirations about school. If we have students from another school, community or country, with whom we can interact and share knowledge, we will all benefit from it. It's an energy charge in terms of possibility and connectivity. The opportunity to share knowledge and information from all around the world really has created a whole new sense of what school is about. It's almost as if you're on a field trip every day. There's a sense that today I might discover something. That sense of discovery is of huge value and part of the initial intent of school and teaching and learning. We sense it and see it with teachers, students, parents, and it has ultimately resulted in more enthusiasm for school.

2.1

Part of the advantage of the electronic and digital world is speed. Through expeditious processing and timely dissemination of information, we may look at student performance not from a period basis but on a regular formative basis, and use differentiated and specific data to drive instructional planning. This has created a blend of the art and science of teaching. For years we've had a sense of the artistry of teaching and the eloquence of the teacher's methodology and sharing concepts and communicating, but now we're blending it with the best of the science in terms of using data, integrating it into planning, and ultimately improving the overall quality of the time spent in the classroom. There's a real energy and excitement about integrating electronic digital tools in the classroom, personalising daily interaction with students based upon specific needs of individuals or groups, and teaching more efficiently and productively.

Ultimately we'll have an IEP[1] for each student. We currently use an IEP online programme for all special-needs students. The concept of having a specialised plan for every student is nothing new, but its efficient processing is new. There certainly is potential, taking full advantage of high-speed Internet, efficient communication and timely electronic data processing to provide teachers and parents with opportunities to communicate about individual student needs, incorporate that in planning for an entire class, and then fine-tune efforts for individual students within that class. Using a more efficient tool set and creating higher levels of productivity saves time. Whether it's part of both a state and national standard in terms of looking at assessments to drive decisions regarding student progress or school accreditation, by using digital

1. Individual Education Plan.

process and electronic means, it creates greater efficiencies. We see that through the assessment tutorial remediation process, efficient review of material by having timely data available, and in efficiencies in the school.

Previously, if a teacher needed to have a study group, there would be an effort to schedule classes, go to the library to look up resources for a particular point of study. With laptops in every classroom, the teacher can do that instantaneously within the room with just a few directives to a group of students or the class. So, there are continuous revelations of efficiencies by using total electronic connectivity that integrates well with accountability systems, whether NCLB[2], state accountability or local accountability. It's imperative at both national and state level that policy-makers develop language that provides flexibility for utilisation of funds; language that previously would have been strictly earmarked for a particular kind of material purchase would now be opened up, as we have seen in Virginia, from initial language referred to strictly as textbooks, but now changed to curriculum materials. This changes both the intent and opportunity for school systems to make purchases.

2. No Child Left Behind. https://nclb.ecs.org/nclb

## Compatible tool-sets

It's extremely relevant to our national prosperity that there's both national and state impetus, encouragement and support for school systems to move in this direction. Whether it's on a national or global basis, students' capabilities of utilising the tool sets they will use in their world of work in their efforts to communicate and prosper as adults simply makes good sense. If we use tool sets that prepare children for a world that no longer exists, it does little to benefit them. It's so important that from a national and local perspective we really understand the importance of providing the same tool sets for school classrooms that we would want in our workplace and for any other type of preparation for work. One of the most exciting elements of our local initiative has been the building of a bridge over the digital divide in the US. On a daily basis we hear, see, sense and know that students are crossing that bridge to a better place for their lives and their families. It's so important that we understand as a community and a country that that bridge must be for all children, not just for those in certain communities. To say that it's important to build that bridge is one thing, to call on a community to join together to build it and endure some of the hardships of building it is something else. Many that may have been quick to verbalise their support in theory were not nearly as supportive when we endured hardships in building that bridge. The greater community believes that that is important and can see the value in it, that it's not a simple process, but the end result is a better place for children, families and communities. It's well worth the effort and the end result will far outweigh the cost of the challenge in building it.

Just as we're seeing new discovery in the classroom, we're also finding it in terms of opportunities for productivity and efficiency. Our homebound instruction is for students unable to attend for whatever reason. Because they have computers, they can access with greater frequency, dependability and more import curriculum information and teacher contact that previously would have been limited and sometimes even impossible. We've also developed programmes that would have been very specialised in our high schools, but through electronic connectivity we can provide that class to students in a variety of high schools, creating human resource efficiency and a sense of a new direction for school. This will result in specialisation and personalisation, which goes back to the curriculum being driven by relevance, interest and importance for students, teachers and parents. Every day we see new possibilities of efficiencies. There's also a sense of equity of all teachers and staff having access, with improved means to communicate with each other after school hours. There are greater opportunities for staff development for continuing their education as they are also taking full advantage of this full bloom of technology for all employees and students.

2.1

'Through electronic connectivity we can provide that class to students in a variety of high schools, creating human resource efficiency and a sense of a new direction for school.'

Some of the previous isolation of teachers is changing. We have developed connectivity both through formal application of staff development and through informal chatrooms, instant messaging, discussion boards, where teachers have a chance to share with and know each other. We hear every day that there's a value in their technical core knowledge of teaching, but also it has added personalisation to their lives as teachers, and a greater sense of community. This initiative is significant and has driven teachers, compelled them to learn from each other. It has also compelled them to want to continue to learn and communicate at a whole different level. We're seeing a sense of vibrancy, a network of connections from teacher to teacher and class to class, sharing information, with new teachers learning from veteran teachers, veterans being invigorated by new teachers' ideas, and a sense of cross-fertilisation previously not possible, diminishing the isolation that previously inhibited teacher productivity.

Some of our clubs have developed web pages for ongoing communication, taking the very best of those programmes. It's exciting to see students, faculties and principals taking advantage of it in the best spirit of helping each other. Students can use it for their economic gain and productivity in the workplace, but there are huge opportunities to use it for community gain and for creating better places for people to live. Hundreds of schools have visited Enrico County looking to emulate what we've done over the past few years and have gone on to start initiatives. Leadership and a sense of possibility have been vital, translated into the daily action of school leaders. To put things in motion takes a sense of urgency: the time is now and the children in our schools are important. We're encouraged by what we're hearing from students, faculty and parents – that it's essential to move forward. The collective will of school leaders will have a huge impact in moving this from an experiment to a way of caring and helping children.

### Flexibility and productivity

Our programme integrates well with local control or psych-based management. One of the benefits of technology in the classroom and of using digital content is flexibility in individual students' needs being serviced. It has benefits for teachers designing work based upon individual productivity and needs. School principals, communities, teachers and students all have greater flexibility in the classroom. In our schools we have significant ESL populations; whereas in the past we had access to a few dictionaries in the classroom, now all students have access to online dictionaries. In addition to print media, we have audio dictionaries available where not just the individual student but families now have access to this resource to help them navigate a new world or navigate a transition into a new community. In schools where we have a greater need, there's an opportunity to differentiate the use of that resource to a whole different level. It links to school-based and class-based initiatives and to principals and teachers designing and using a resource based upon particular needs rather than just a generic resource model that one size fits all.

'The efficiency and the navigation process of literacy and of learning has been improved and enhanced dramatically by 21st-century tools.'

As a school system we spend approximately $500 less per pupil than the state average, and even though we're a good resource system, we're still operating in terms of a state comparison at a moderate level of expenditure. We've seen many poorer school districts aligning their resource towards the future, and have been able to deploy a one-to-one model to students using a percentage of their operating budget, by making choices about how resources will be used. By moving in this direction we no longer have to make purchases for a lot of period resource materials we would have bought individually. We're able to provide student access to a whole array of media information services where previously we would have bought individual hard copies. We no longer do interim report cards to students in hard copy: we do it online, resulting in real expenditure reduction. We no longer use classroom space for computer labs. In a growing district like Enrico, capital space is very important: we currently have 40–50 classrooms previously used as labs and freed up for regular classrooms, resulting in multimillion dollar savings. We've improved our point-of-contact service, but instead of investing in more people to go out, we're providing a higher level of contact by using online services.

Our elementary students today are well prepared for computing. We've glimpsed it with individual elementary schools having a rolling lab, and schools that have purchased laptop computers and placed them in classrooms have increased their productivity. In our elementary classrooms desktop computers and their level of utilisation translates well to laptops. When we introduced them to sixth graders we were apprehensive, but they've probably done as well as any grade level, maybe even better. The same would be true for third, fourth or fifth graders. Whether we go below third grade, I believe, would be debatable. I will tell you a significant number of second-grade teachers would be very disappointed, but ultimately that's a future decision, and there are no current plans to move in that direction. But as a matter of personal professional reference, I would certainly advocate it.

2.1

Overall use of technology is improving literacy. When we look at the role of educational materials in creating and enhancing literacy, we have over the years evolved from primary resources into the use of technology, and now have specialised programmes meeting individual student needs with data integration as part of it. But we also see evidence daily, because of the relevance of broad and timely information, a greater interest in students retrieving, accessing and seeking information, whether the reading material is traditional or related to other core content areas. In terms of the writing process, because of the utilitarian advantage of using a word processor, students are much more inclined to write. Our English teachers say students write more often, understand editing at a whole different level, and enjoy the process more. It's not as cumbersome and it makes good sense. Ultimately, the efficiency and the navigation process of literacy and of learning has been improved and enhanced dramatically by 21st-century tools.

# Student-centred learning: making an aircraft carrier dance

**John English** I Community Superintendent, Fairfax County, US

**Student-centred learning reflects the intention to customise the classroom experience for each student. John English discusses Fairfax's phenomenal success in harnessing technology to break down the barriers around the schooling process and to encourage lifelong learning.**

The student-centred classroom is gaining momentum and creating positive school changes as a result of shifts in teaching style, teaching approaches, and professional practices of educators. For many years in classrooms, the teacher stood in front of the class doing most of the talking, while students took notes and were tested to show they remembered about what the teacher had said or had assigned. It is now known through brain research and other educational studies that the person doing the talking is the person doing the learning. Educational best practice is no longer teachers being entertained by the sound of their own voice. Increasingly teachers are evolving to be the coach at the side of students and working to personalise the learning experience.

There was a time when it was thought that education was for status, economic advancement and self-satisfaction to have a better, happier life. Now education is viewed as a process of joining a community of learners – not only for the student but also for teachers, parents and the community at large. There are still the educational goals of taking challenging courses and moving on to colleges and universities for economic advantage as well as stimulation, but education is becoming more communal in terms of learning success. Education used to be the students acting alone, trying to learn and compete against other students. It was basic competitive learning. Now the learning experience is far more collaborative. The benefits obviously accrue to an individual student, but also to other students and the teachers in the learning community.

To achieve student-centred learning the classroom has to be organised and led by the teacher who continuously assesses learning outcomes and at the same time works to match a teaching style to individual student learning styles. To personalise that learning, the teacher must be far more sophisticated in making professional decisions. The mission is not just to fill empty vessels with profound knowledge. The overall goal is to teach students to learn how to learn.

We used to think each student's ability determined how much was learned, but that was actually a measure of how fast you could learn something.

People with high IQs learned quickly, those with low IQs learned more slowly. Now we know the learning process is more complex, and that if we can customise the learning experience, the speed of learning is not as important as the process to ensure that learning actually takes place and advances for all learners. Of course it's a more complicated process for teachers because students are learning different things at different rates. When teachers construct the meaning together with an individual or group of students, the learning is far more permanent for the students. Howard Gardner at Harvard is fond of saying, 'It is not how smart you are that matters; it is how are you smart and what you do when you do not know the answer to a problem?'

2.2

## Training and retraining teachers

To promote change or progress in the classroom, it is vital to constantly train and retrain veteran staff as well as new hires. There was a time when pre-service teachers completed their practice teaching and then were hired into the profession as a fully fledged teacher. Now it is generally acknowledged that teachers must continue practising their profession until the day they retire. Beginning teachers need at least three years of support if they are to succeed, so it is important to establish a beginning teachers' support system. Basically it is a system of veteran teachers training beginner teachers to teach in more sophisticated and successful ways. Most teachers tend to teach the way they were taught. To break that cycle, and to build on new findings from educational research and practices, constant retraining and professional development are made available throughout the career of a teacher.

When new teachers come onboard they are provided with the full suite of equipment that they need to be successful. We made the decision last year that although all our K-6, middle-school and high-school teachers had desktop units, we needed to move to the next level of access. We're now at the point where we issue teachers a high-end wireless laptop so they can use it throughout school, take it home and have web access so that they can more easily organise their work. So the initiative includes the hardware, software and, of course, ongoing staff training.

As more successful practices evolve in the classroom, there must be continuous connects between parents and teachers. In the past, the only connection between home and school was the student, who would come home and describe what went on at school and then come back to school the next day and describe what went on with their homework at home. Parents would get quarterly report cards and an occasional phone call or letter if something serious was happening at school. Communication about what is expected to be learned, how the student is doing and what's going to be taught next or what needs to be re-taught was generally left for the student to communicate between parents and teachers.

## Shifts in educational practices

| Diminishing practices |  | Evolving practices |
|---|---|---|
| • Natural selection theory | | • Talent can be developed |
| • Excellence for a few | | • Excellence for all |
| • Remedial programs | | • Early prevention |
| • Pessimism about learning | | • Optimism about learning |
| • Competitive learning | | • Cooperative learning |
| • Exclusive programmes | | • Inclusive programmes |
| • Mystery learning | | • Mastery learning |
| • Fear | | • Trust |
| • Failure syndrome | | • Success ethos |
| • Deficit comments | | • Validation phrases |
| • Focus on incorrect responses | | • Focus on approximations of correct responses |
| • Teacher as taskmaster | | • Teacher as leader of learners |

Educators are beginning to build an open environment for the future as assessment strategies evolve to inform instruction. Giving the test at the end of the unit, course or year is often too late for certain learners. The teacher (and parents) find out students didn't learn it, but it's too late. I call that finding autopsy data because the course or unit is over. We can now get instant feedback with online assessment, where students can say, 'I've learned this much and I need to learn the next piece to move on'. The assessment is more formative and diagnostic and keeps the learner and teacher in touch with where they are in the unit of study. This results in a change in the dynamic connection among the learner, parents, and teachers.

### Connecting communities

We're just starting to connect family, community members and experts with the classroom. We're implementing the use of an online programme called the FCPS (Fairfax County Public Schools) 24/7 home-school portal. It's an electronic communication tool designed especially for teachers, students and parents for individual courses. Although its use began mostly at the university level, it has had significant impact at our K-12 schools as well. FCPS 24/7 (aka Blackboard) is clearly one of the great potentials being tapped to develop a community of learners rather than just an isolated classroom. With the portal in place, the virtual community becomes a vital part of the whole learning experience, not just for experts in the community, but also students and certainly parents. When parents, teachers and students are continuously connected, the learning is greatly enhanced. The process of teaching and learning happens more quickly and deeply and it's a better experience for everyone.

The idea of student-centred learning in a connected community is sensible. Students often think that grades happen to them because the teacher controls the grade book and only allows students and parents to see it four times a year. Even in terms of attendance in school – the students believe school is responsible for their attendance because all the data is kept in the attendance office. With students and parents being able to view their grades on a regular basis as well as attendance, discipline, and curriculum objectives, they can take far more control of their own learning, and they accept more responsibility for the schooling process. Responsibility can be viewed as two words, not just one: students have the *ability* to choose how they *respond* to all learning situations. They certainly have the ability to decide whether they are going to attend class and what their grades will be by how much effort they put into the learning process. So students and parents become far more in control of learning as a result of having information about their learning on a regular 24/7 basis.

2.2

'When parents, teachers and students are continuously connected, the learning is greatly enhanced. The process of teaching and learning happens more quickly and deeply and it's a better experience for everyone.'

Blackboard has only been available for a few years now and there's a wide range of use among the early adaptors. Teachers all give student assignments. Most teachers are starting to post assignments on a daily, weekly, sometimes monthly basis, but teachers have also turned it into a virtual classroom where, whether students are in school, at home or on vacation, they can log into their virtual classroom, be part of text discussions with other students, submit work to their teacher as a draft and the teacher can comment on it and send it back to them for final version. The worst part about schooling was when you needed something – usually either when the school day was over, when the classroom was being used for another purpose or when the teacher was unavailable. Through the Blackboard virtual classroom, many such obstacles are removed. It's not instantaneous real-time communication, but it's certainly a communication vehicle never before available to teachers, learners and parents.

### Achievement for all

On another front, educators have moved from the idea of sorting and selecting which students advance their learning to the goal of having every student complete high-school education to the best of their ability. The economy, the politics and certainly the goals of education have shifted dramatically. At one point, 50 years ago, not having a highly educated workforce was an economic benefit. People could find work in factory jobs doing fairly mundane things over and over again; large farms could employ many people. That has all changed. Not finishing high school is an economic liability, not only to the student but also to the economy. Obviously the goal of educators now is to have all students graduate with high standards of learning; in some cases we are approaching that fairly dramatically. With local and state accountability systems, there is strong evidence that not only are students passing the courses, but it is also possible to measure what have learned.

---

## 'Not finishing high school is an economic liability, not only to the student but also to the economy.'

---

For most of the past in public education, the question was how to get access to learning for certain learners, people of different races, people with handicaps, irrespective of gender. It was about access to learning by getting in the schoolhouse door and in the classroom, but it was never a question that, once you were there, would actual learning take place. And then when we started all the standardised testing, we were looking at mean or average scores and could virtually mask the fact that Fairfax has high test scores. If you just disaggregate the results by the different subgroups, you will find that some subgroups need more attention and resources and teaching to be brought up to the same level as the other learners.

Fairfax educators have created a data warehouse so teachers and administrators can actually track individual learners, groups of learners and subgroups of learners by whatever category you want to put them into. If we want to know how the Hispanic male students in the 9th grade are doing in Algebra 1, we look at that kind of disaggregation. It was the creation of this data warehouse that gave us real-time information. We don't wait till the end of the year, we do it each marking period so we have far more data upfront to support our decisions. We are not there yet, we haven't gotten that far, but our initiatives are triggering those kinds of sophisticated processes.

The next phase is to make parents aware of their student's progress. Right now on our Blackboard accounts, parents have to enter through their student's password because Blackboard was invented for universities. That's where we were using it most. So now we bring it to the K-12 arena, and are creating a portal where parents have their own password and can see certain kinds of information related to their own sons and daughters. Students of course would have their password, they could see certain kinds of information, and even teachers and administrators would have access to information, all on a need-to-know basis.

As a lifelong learner I know teachers as well as students have to be taught to be learners. Certain people adapt quickly and others hold back and say, 'I can't do this,' or 'I don't want to do this' or 'I'll never do that.' So one technique we use in our schools is that teachers are allowed to put themselves in their own group. They can be a rabbit or a turtle: a rabbit's going to go out really quickly and adapt and make a lot of mistakes but learn fairly quickly; turtles are going to come behind and figure out what works for them. But as a leader in a school, I would tell them in September that it's certainly OK if you don't know how to use Blackboard right now because you're new to the system, but if you're not using it by after Christmas, then we have a problem. If you're not using it by the end of the school year, then you probably might want to look for another place to work.

## Plan for school improvement

For other school systems trying to get to where we are, the first thing is to operate from a plan. It doesn't have to be a step-by-step plan, but you've got to have a vision, expectations and a way of charting what's working and what's helping kids. Secondly, you need 'organised abandonment'. You're going to have to make hard choices. Our budgets don't grow by significant amounts from year to year. The best we can do is raise some salaries and build a few more classrooms. Organised abandonment means the end of high-cost, low-impact traditional kinds of work, in order to free up the venture capital to move into the next successful phase of how we do our business. Blackboard and better access to date are part of this next phase. Those are tough decisions because sometimes teachers don't support it, sometimes parents don't, and sometimes it's hard to get Boards to understand the vision. Therefore, a plan must be clear, precise, and realistic. The FCPS 24/7 plan is a good example of this practice:

2.2

- Secure the commitment and involvement of community stakeholders – students, teachers, administrators, parents, higher education faculty, and business and industry leaders – in the implementation of the K12nects II Stuart Pyramid Schools programme.

- Provide universal, web-based access to integrated curricula and high-quality resources that are aligned with the FCPS Programmes of Study, the Virginia Standards of Learning, and national educational goals.

- Develop new qualitative and quantitative assessment tools that are aligned with these standards and which allow data-driven decision-making.

- Deploy new computing devices (desktop and wireless computers, web appliances, and/or other), multiple points of secure Internet access, the necessary server technology, and a variety of communications options throughout all Stuart Pyramid schools.

- Demonstrate an increase in learning and academic achievement for every student.

- Secure additional full-time positions for site-based technology trainers and technical support personnel at each pyramid school.

- Provide teacher training in the design and implementation of technology-supported instruction.

- Provide recurrent opportunities for teachers to collaborate as members of interdisciplinary teams and vertically, K-12.

- Provide teacher training in the assessment of student progress and achievement.

- Ensure that neither gender, race, ethnicity, socio-economic status nor ability is a barrier to access to learning.

- Extend community-wide access beyond the traditional school day and environment.

- Provide secure parent access to students' schedules, attendance, progress, and grades.

- Promote 24/7 parent-teacher communication through the use of e-mail and school websites.

- Provide graduate-level courses to administrators and teachers in the use of technology as an instructional tool.

- Obtain authentic work experiences for students and teachers with local industries.

- Procure hardware, software, technical assistance, and financial support from partner corporations.

- Serve as a model for private sector/public education partnerships.

Change in education is like changing the course of an aircraft carrier: there are so many different parts and so many people involved. Improvements must be thought out and well planned, but not doing anything tends toward stagnation and not getting the expected results. To make an aircraft carrier dance like a PT boat, the key element is intention: always pushing continuous improvements. When I was principal of a high-performing high school, my mantra was that good schools can only remain good schools as long as they are improving their service, their results and student learning. The intention must be to always examine educational practices. For a long time education suffered from 'unexamined practice'. Institutionalised ways of doing business have a tendency to remain in place regardless of benefit. So we examine our practices, we question ourselves and make ourselves vulnerable to outsiders to do the same. Some people think that resources improve education. My sense is that intention leads to improvements which changes education. The resources follow a well-intended plan.

2.2

# Spreading the message

**Toine Maes** | General Manager of Kennisnet, The Netherlands

**Toine Maes discusses how Kennisnet's activities are helping to shape the future of education in the Netherlands by creating a more focused, relevant search engine (Davindi) and standardising classification of content (metadata) to harness the power of Internet content.**

Kennisnet was founded two-and-a-half years ago as an Internet organisation and is run as an education foundation for the Dutch education sector, covering primary, secondary and professional education. Its aim is to develop the best products and services for the sector and, at an earlier stage, to ensure that all schools are connected to the Internet. We try to provide schools with as much content as they want from publishers, organisations or individual people in the Netherlands and we do so through an educational portal allowing every teacher, student, parent and manager in the education sector to extract what they want from it.

My background is in economics; after graduating I worked in the Ministry of Education and Science and became Director of Technology Policy within the Ministry of Economic Affairs. My involvement in education began after it was decided that the ministry needed to be involved more in education. The minister asked me to set up a separate education department and, after doing this, I joined the umbrella organisation for cable companies in the Netherlands. The cable sector had won the contract for connecting all schools to the Internet and having done this job for four years I was asked to take responsibility for Kennisnet, becoming general manager in early 2001.

I developed my vision on education further with Kennisnet, because I had the chance to become involved with the education sector and the problems within it, far more intensely than previously. The past three or four years have enabled me to develop my own perspective on how education might evolve during the coming five to ten years.

What I've seen is that the demand for education is becoming far more complex than ten or twenty years ago. That's not because people are different, but because the situations, for example in the Netherlands, are different. We have more people coming from abroad to settle in the Netherlands which is influencing the demand for education. Moreover, while people born in Holland now acknowledge the differences between learners, we are still using one standard method of teaching. The challenge for education is not for the demand

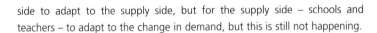

side to adapt to the supply side, but for the supply side – schools and teachers – to adapt to the change in demand, but this is still not happening.

One way of teaching, and of organising, developing and building schools is no longer good enough. We need to be transparent and flexible, and to have a toolbox in which schools and teachers have many more instruments they can use to teach with instead of just putting a teacher in front of a classroom. This is the challenge that has driven me to be involved in education. How can you get a system that has changed very little over 150 years to change in such a way that learners are provided with more flexible ways of learning; away from dependency on time and place; with more flexible learning from home; mobile learning; or whatever learning they want? The system should adapt and give them these possibilities.

2.3

To pursue this vision, we need a period of educational innovation in which IT and ICT are regarded as crucial. If you are an Internet organisation, knowing that the Internet is one of the instruments that can make education as flexible as possible, then the challenge for Kennisnet is to become one of those instruments in the toolbox of every teacher and learner. This will enable them to incorporate the Internet into the education system so that they can access it at anytime and anywhere – not to replace the teacher or the traditional system, but to add another way of teaching and learning. This takes a lot of work, because first you have to teach the basic skills in how to use IT before teachers can start using it. It involves a change from 'learning to use' to 'using to learn' – a change that is needed within the main core of teachers.

### Davindi: crossing the threshold

The second phase is for teachers to learn to use IT in the classroom. The way we do this is not to focus on IT per se, but instead to focus on the content that IT can bring us: brilliant content, which has the potential to broaden all of our horizons and yet be highly accessible, and – most importantly – genuinely current in that it can be updated overnight. If you can trigger teachers' interest so that they regain the original enthusiasm that attracted them to becoming teachers in the first place – literally to spread content and the understanding of it among learners – they become even more enthusiastic if you give them another tool to spread that content. When they see how effective this content is, they will be motivated to change their approach and to adapt the way in which they use IT.

It's not easy or natural for older teachers to use the Internet, so we have to encourage them to cross the threshold. Rather than focusing on all the IT skills they have to learn before they can start, we need to show them how useful the content is and how using IT can make their job as a teacher enjoyable again. To achieve this, in 2001 we initiated large projects with commercial and educational publishers in the Netherlands to develop a huge variety of web-based content for our portal – content that can't be found anywhere else on the Internet or through resources such as Google. All of this is dedicated to the education sector and can be accessed through Kennisnet.

Secondly, although we encourage the use of search engines, such as Yahoo or Google, we have developed another way of searching specifically for the education sector – which we prefer to call a 'find engine'. The reason for doing so is that if you search, say, Google and you're not precise enough, you will get a million or more search results. If a teacher is interested in a topic, then a million search results creates such a big lake that they will not be able to swim in it. Our find engine, called Davindi – combining the inspiration of Leonardo da Vinci with vindi, the Dutch word for find – produces a more manageable number of Internet links with greater relevance to the education sector.

We prefer to call it the 'find engine' because the unique selling point should be that you only get only those search results which are of genuine educational value. That's why Kennisnet developed partnerships with several other organisations within the Netherlands such as libraries, public broadcasters and educational publishers, to enrich the Davindi engine with as much content with educational value as we can get. A particular search will give a mix of results such as links to websites, streaming video clips, games etc. We have very high expectations of this new type of 'find engine', especially in its ability to be far more precise than conventional search engines and in delivering a more acceptable number of results.

Davindi has been developed in conjunction with 2000 teachers across the Netherlands and with the country's libraries to provide added value to the education system. It now has some 60,000 links, which have all been researched and classified by teachers themselves. It's easy for a teacher to add a link: all they have to do is fill in a template; give the web address; write three of four lines on what a teacher or student can find there, whether it's in Dutch or English; and rate it on a scale of one to five stars, just like on the Amazon site.

We have about 50 professional communities, all of which have a manager – one for history, one for geography, arithmetic, science etc – each of whom look after their own community. The managers select the teachers who make up their community, looking for innovators who are heavily involved with the Internet and know how to search it well. Every year we ask them to provide so many links and they get paid for every link they put into the system.

Usage numbers are exploding and the portal and find engine together now attract some 600,000 unique visitors every week. These are mainly Dutch users, because most of the content is in Dutch, although we aim to translate the whole portal into English.

> 'We're looking into every aspect of the content chain and how we can create even more innovative projects out of it.'

In terms of how it is being used, there is evidence that students come to the classroom and say that they have already looked on Davindi, have found certain information and have shown it to the teacher. This creates a far more interactive way of learning, which is what we want – and the Internet is the main instrument for this. We are about to introduce similar communities and community managers for students and learners and are deciding whether they should use the same form that the teachers use or one created especially for them.

2.3

### Metadata and the educational content chain

Another initiative in progress is the standardisation of meta-tagging and classification of our content – a large project called Metadata, which is focusing specifically on the vocational sector. This includes a national exercise to build a profile of vocabularies and the fields you have to fill in to search. This is to be tested so that it can become the Dutch standard for meta-tagging in the education sector and can be expanded to cover content for primary and secondary schools.

Out of the Metadata project, we have formulated a much larger innovation project called the educational content chain. This focuses not only on meta-tagging, because that's just one step, but on the whole content chain. It is examining what phases are necessary to get content from a developer to the end user and is looking at open standards, technical platforms for providing content and the concept of content stimulation. We're looking into every aspect of the content chain and how we can create even more innovative projects out of it.

### The connected school

While the Kennisnet portal and Davindi have added a whole new dimension of online content to education in Netherlands, there will still be a need for students to attend schools and it's important that this social component of education is not undervalued. You need group processes to provide good education. In the future, pupils will go to a school or similar place, which may not be organised in the same way as it is now. Often the most innovative changes take place in new schools and the provision of new designs for school buildings is another way of stimulating innovation in education.

It is also likely that there will be fewer divisions and that teaching groups will become bigger, with more teachers for each group. This will solve the problem of teacher shortages and staff sickness, as the group will not rely on a single teacher and have to be sent home if they are absent. With greater use of the Internet, the teacher becomes more of a coach than a figure standing in front of a classroom.

---

'If you want to keep good teachers, you have to give them a sense of greater opportunities and prospects.'

---

Already, in the Netherlands, teaching assistants play an important role in supporting teachers, so that they can spend more time teaching and coaching and have more contact with their students. This enables them to focus more on the process of teaching and helping students to acquire a good education. There is often a team of staff for each group of students, not just one teacher.

This is also a very important issue in management development, because one potentially disturbing factor in becoming a teacher is the thought that you'll be the same teacher when you are 60 as you were when you started at the age of 25. The lack of opportunity for growth and management development is a major factor for many teachers who reach the age of 40 and decide to leave the profession. If you want to keep good teachers, you have to give them a sense of greater opportunities and prospects and this is one way to do that.

As for accessing the Internet, I personally believe that every student should have a laptop, equipped with all the necessary software, learning tools and easy Internet access. I know, however, that this is very costly and it will take years to realise this, so for the coming five to ten years students will probably depend on the vision of their particular school. There may be an open learning centre or a few computers in every classroom – it will depend on how schools want to use the technology and integrate it into their school vision.

Already we are seeing innovative schools where every student has a laptop, but those are very rare at the moment. There is still a big debate on how to use computers in the classroom and where they should be located, so that they can be used in the most effective and efficient ways. As yet, there is no consensus on this.

Such fundamental changes in the way that future education is organised and delivered will have far-reaching effects on the assessment of educational standards and measuring of student attainment. There is no national curriculum in the Netherlands and, although the law states that the education system is free to choose how education services are delivered, it does have to ensure that certain standards are achieved. How to assess achievement still has to be addressed. Certain new school projects are developing new teaching systems without organising students into traditional groups and the first challenge this creates is how to develop new assessment and inspection procedures to replace those of the old system. They still have to take part in the existing national assessment procedures, but are looking at how they can be more flexible and apply greater use of computers and the Internet to achieve this.

### The role of government

Although all these changes impact on national education policy, government policy is generally becoming less important, because, if you believe in professionals and professional institutions, then they must be able to do their job without interference. They should accept guidance from their customers, but not from government. I believe the government's role should be to set the framework, in the sense of rules and budgets, and to stimulate innovation that is too big to be dealt with by individual institutions themselves. For example, the government should be concerned with connecting all the schools with broadband access to the Internet. This level of innovation is impossible for schools to handle themselves and must be dealt with in the first phase of introduction on a national scale.

2.3

The government should be introducing innovation into the school system and leave the schools to handle their individual product innovation. A manager of a school has to develop their product – education – and sell it to its customers – learners and their parents. National and local government should be looking at areas such as infrastructure and how to provide broadband, fibre optic or wireless Internet access for all schools. On the content side, they should look to organisations, such as Kennisnet, to develop more innovative content for schools across the country.

One of the biggest improvements that we can deliver is to provide students with easy access to content that is accurate and up-to-date. In the Netherlands, there are still schools that use textbooks that talk about guilders, not euros. I'm not saying that books will stop playing a part in the school system, but web content complements them with more up-to-date information. If you look at a map of Europe, you will see how much has changed over the past ten years and, in my view, it is unacceptable for schools to be using atlases showing Europe as it was in 1990 when we are now in 2004.

The time it can take publishers to develop new materials can be very frustrating. Sometimes it can take a few years for primary education materials to be developed, which will then be used in the classroom for about eight years. So the actual figures and context can be 10–12 years out of date. This is a wasted opportunity when you consider we have such a powerful instrument as the Internet, which enables you to change content every day or whenever you require. It is also unbelievable that many people still don't have a clue about how much the Internet can influence the quality of education for the better.

# Relevant, reliable and risk-free

**John Anderson** | Education Technology Strategy Coordinator,
Northern Ireland School Service
**Jimmy Stewart** | Director of the C2K Project, Northern Ireland

John Anderson and Jimmy Stewart talk about the rapid changes taking place in the Northern Ireland education system, where the Classroom 2000 Project (C2K) supports the educational technology strategy and provides a managed service solution. It has become a model for a centralised approach to ICT resourcing in schools, of interest across the world.

Education in Northern Ireland is a devolved responsibility and, even with the Northern Ireland Assembly currently suspended, government policy derives less and less from policy in England than before. We are seeing a variety of different answers to the same problems emerge across the U.K. The implementation of Classroom 2000 (C2K) and the Northern Ireland Education Technology Strategy[1] can best be understood in the context of the Labour government's National Grid for Learning[2] (NGfL) policy. C2K in Northern Ireland turned out to be a more complete implementation of what Stevenson[3] intended of NGfL, than you might find elsewhere. As a small education service we are more easily able to innovate in the education service and to provide a dynamic service.

## Origins of C2K

C2K grew out of an organisation called CLASS, established in 1991. It was a regional solution to provide management information systems (MIS) services across all schools. Each school had its own standalone MIS network. There was no interface between these networks and the authority's business process network. We're only now just getting to grips with integration into the Education and Library Boards (the equivalent of the local authorities in England and Wales) and the Department of Education's infrastructures and this is one of the processes C2K will be undertaking.

The original strategy had four elements: to review the curriculum and to embed the use of technology in learning; to look at teacher development to ensure we had a competent workforce with a view to improving classroom practice. To deliver that output in the classroom we need to have the final two elements in place – the infrastructure and communication services that will allow teachers to take full advantage of the technologies coming on stream. C2K's role in the strategy is to provide a fully distributed infrastructure across all 1200 schools in Northern Ireland; to connect those schools together into a secure, wide area environment; and to resource that service with content that is both relevant to the curriculum and up-to-date in terms of its use of modern

1. The Northern Ireland Education Technology Strategy can be found at http://www.deni.gov.uk/aboutstrategies/d–ets.htm The most recent government strategy is at http://www.empoweringschools.com

2. Details of the National Grid for Learning can be found at http://www.ngfl.gov.uk

3. Stevenson, D. (1997). Information and Communications Technology in UK Schools. An Independent Inquiry. London: The Independent ICT in Schools Commission.

technologies. Therefore C2K's role from 1998 onwards was to put in place the contracts that would deliver those services in the schools.

Some of the schools have been using technology for nearly 20 years; some had standalone machines while in others there were computer suites and they were connected by dial-up to the Internet. We recognised that if we were to embed ICT in classroom practice, we needed to have machines in every classroom, so the aspiration in Northern Ireland was to move to a greater distribution across the school. Certainly there would be suites of computers in schools but C2K's role was not to provide these but to provide a distributed network in every school to make sure that they each had at least one or two workstations in each classroom that would be available for teachers to use when they wanted, and that the pupils would be able to access systems when needed without having to timetable that into a programme. The central funding provided for an average of one PC for every ten pupils distributed over the primary and post-primary sectors so that primary schools had one PC to 11 pupils, and the secondary ratio was one to eight.

2.4

### Curriculum developments

The curriculum element of C2K links in with the current revision of the curriculum which is putting learning processes and skills competence development at its core. We are trying to move to a view of the curriculum where subjects are seen as contexts in which common core skills, competences and processes are developed across the school. People are becoming more comfortable with the language of *learning* which is a much better currency than the language of *curriculum* in describing what we want to achieve and to support through learning technology to make education more suited for the twenty-first century.

The statutory requirements have been reduced significantly in order to give teachers more freedom, end of Key Stage tests will be phased out. Schools must report to parents on the development of a range of competencies and skills through a pupil profile. One expects to find literacy and numeracy at the heart, but there are also will be personal competences like critical and creative thinking, the ability to work in a team, and to be more individually self-reliant in learning.

The biggest change will be to move away from selection at the age of 11, by 2008, and to replace it with a curriculum entitlement, at the age of 14 where every pupil must have access to a choice of 24 courses at least one-third to be vocational and one-third academic. At the age of 16 that menu must have at least 27 courses with flexibility for the introduction of additional courses to suit individual schools.

While we have a small service we have many types of schools: grammar schools, non-selective schools, integrated schools, Irish medium schools. Some are mainly Catholic and some Protestant. Any market town has a range of smaller schools with limited curriculum choice and diversity to match their individual needs. There are few schools in Northern Ireland which can deliver the full entitlement on its own so they will need to get together with schools in their neighbourhood and their local college for further education to form a partnership.

> 'There's little point in moving to a greater emphasis on using technology in learning unless it's matched by major developments in assessment.'

It is intended that schools may develop specialisms: for instance academic, or in the performing arts, or in agriculture, or in music or technology. By working together, schools will be able to share their particular expertise across the pupil range that exists in all the schools in that partnership. The technology is expected to support collaboration through text and video conferencing, applications sharing facilities, and so on within Learning NI, our e-learning platform. It will allow an expert in one school to work with generalist teachers in another school to deliver courses to a much broader range of pupils than would have been the case in the past. We ought be able to continue to live with our relatively small schools, supporting their local community, but working together to provide a much richer curriculum than at the moment.

Province-wide we have two major policy initiatives of curriculum reform and structural reform. A timetable has been put in place and there are moves to test out partnership arrangements. C2K provides the vehicle to support quite significant changes in education at three levels. At the classroom level it will focus on personalising the experience for every child. At the school level we're trying to provide effective managed information – information enabling managers to make decisions about what's good and not so good about their schools, and to give them a service that's absolutely dependable and sustainable in the foreseeable future. The third level is the technology that enables changes to take place.

We can only now dare to think that we could offer access to a greater diversity of courses through an online learning environment because we've got the technology to do it. We can also dare to think that we can have fitness for purpose in our service, because there's little point in moving to a greater emphasis on using technology in learning unless it's matched by major developments in assessment. There's enough technology in place in Northern Ireland to realise that it's not really about the technology, instead we can begin to think about the real issues of new approaches to learning. The technology should become transparent because it should become an enabler, helping us do the things we want to do. The objective is to take the technology off the agenda so that it's no longer a part of what we want to do; it's just there so you can use it to do other things.

We are making progress in using technology to bring experts online to teach on a number of subjects as a common resource. Sometimes they are recorded on video, sometimes they're live, and sometimes they're on limited-time hot seats. That's not a challenge or a threat, but enrichment. Most teachers welcome it because it's another rich resource that engages the pupils; it makes teaching much more lively and interesting for everybody. Some teachers are beginning to understand the difference and the change in role relationship that can occur online where a pupil knows something and can contribute to the debate. This seems to be less of a threat to the teacher's authority role when it happens online.

2.4

## **Moving teachers forward**

The fact that pupils have a very high level of access at home and the fact that so many do use the technology as part of their homework, were important factors in getting teachers to use the technology. Pupils, disappointed by their experience of school, seem to be a driver for change. We passed the point a few years back where teachers realised that pupils were bringing expectations into the classroom about the way teachers would teach, and how they would allow them to learn. Pupils have expectations about the extent to which teachers will allow them to engage in Net-based research, to present their new knowledge in multimedia format, and communicate with others elsewhere. Their expectations became a lever for each school, and this came at the point when there was a critical mass of teachers doing interesting things with technology.

Giving every teacher access to a laptop was also part of the process, and the teacher education element of the Education Technology Strategy required teachers to have access while taking part in training. We didn't have the C2K infrastructure fully in place at that stage so we procured around 12,000 laptops – two for every three teachers. They were owned, and are still owned, by the schools. We delivered them to the schools and let the schools deploy them across their teaching workforce as the teachers went through programmes of professional development. The laptops were moved from teacher to teacher depending on who was participating in the programme at any particular time. In reality though, once a teacher got their hands on a laptop they didn't want to give it up. So now we want to provide every teacher with a laptop. Even back in 2000 when we supplied the original kit, some forward thinking schools brought the ratio up to one-to-one by using funds from their own delegated budgets.

Our scheme gives machines to schools that are connected to the infrastructure of the school but which can also be taken home. One of C2K's roles is to supply that core infrastructure and to resource it effectively. In our next major procurement we'll look at providing a managed service solution for every teacher.

Over the past six months secondary schools have had access to managed services and there is now Internet access in every classroom. It's a very fast, 2MB broadband link, and where schools have invested in interactive whiteboards, there's much visibility of the technology. The teachers have harvested the Internet: they've found learning objects, pulled them together into new resources area on their local area network. Their purpose for doing so was straightforward; so that when they wanted to teach a topic they could find a range of objects they could use to help make different concepts easier to explain. It didn't take them long, looking at the menus of learning objects they'd collected in an environment that was open and accessible to everybody to realise that learning objects had the potential to be used by pupils as part of their coursework. You could almost see the light dawn. They had set out to make their teaching job easier and suddenly they had created a learning resource. Students are now using learning objects in their projects – that's the shift that's happening; we want to see what difference it makes.

## A managed service

Our overall responsibility was to take the risk and uncertainty out of technology deployment in the schools. The biggest problem in effectively embedding technology in teaching is still the reliability and sustainability of the service over time for the school. The rationale behind using a centralist approach and providing the C2K service was to remove that problem from the individual schools. We have a ten-year programme running in Northern Ireland, with committed funding from the Department of Education to maintain it, which means that over maybe three incarnations of technology, schools can be absolutely certain that the service is going to be there and that the technology is developed. It means school managers don't have to make the decision as to which direction they take on their technology purchases because that problem has been delivered back into the private sector. Technology enhancement will therefore be in the hands of those who understand where it's going, so allowing teachers to concentrate on teaching and learning, rather than having to worry about whether the technology is going to work.

We've now had the managed service in primary schools for two-and-a-half years. The computers we're putting into classrooms are managed computers, maintained at very high levels. Because of the way we contract, unavailability or under-performance are penalised in terms of the payment mechanism, so service providers have significant incentives to make sure that the systems are running all the time. We're getting well over 99.9% availability on the system, which means that there's virtually no downtime and a teacher can therefore absolutely rely on their system working.

A recent survey showed that teachers' satisfaction responses to that service were higher than expected. There are a number of explanations. Previously teachers didn't feel comfortable with the technology when it didn't work. Primary schools don't have technicians to fix it, so often it stayed broken. Now for the first time primary school teachers are been able to turn to the computer and know it will work and that, when it doesn't, it will be fixed within hours. That's absolutely crucial. The managed service has transformed teachers' confidence and improved their willingness and ability to plan to use ICT in their teaching. Teachers will not embed ICT in their lesson plans unless they are certain it's going to work every time.

---

'You could almost see the light dawn.
They had set out to make their teaching job easier
and suddenly they had created a learning resource.'

---

2.4

C2K has also given teachers a considerable number of educational resources to use and advisers, who support teachers in the classroom, are able to concentrate their efforts on developing resources and recommending titles they know will be of benefit to every teacher. Previously that work was fragmented, because different decisions were made about titles by local authorities and by teachers themselves. Those decisions are still being made in addition but, in a common core, everyone's game has been raised and teachers' attention is turning to the quality of learning. Children's creativity; the quality and focus of their learning; and their competence in ICT learning are measurably increasing. Very recently we visited schools as part of the research for our education technology excellence awards; some of the best primary practice was observed and the quality of pupil's Internet based research was excellent. Higher, in fact, among 10 or 11 year olds than among the 14 year olds in some of our secondary schools, which were later in getting the service. Their rollout started in November 2003 and in just six months we have observed some remarkably good practice.

Within the next year we'll be creating better warehouse facilities, allowing information that resides within the schools to be exported – held in a repository – which will then be available for use within the Library Boards system. This is being built on what C2K has delivered as part of its wide-area service. This is going to make it much easier for the Library Boards to get information and data without teachers having to spend hours on it. At the moment we're producing snapshots for the library boards. Approximately once a year there is a major survey or major census taken and that information is then used by the Library Boards throughout the year. But with this new system they will be able to access live data through an automatic process that will not require any significant resource. So we're moving to a situation that should remove, or significantly reduce, the administrative burden on schools as well as producing management information for the broader service.

We haven't been particularly ambitious or aggressive in terms of our expectations of what these systems will do to help reduce the bureaucratic burden, yet we recognise that there is huge value in a coherent service – a common service, being delivered across 1,200 schools. It isn't just about value for money. Delivery of the managed service to individual institutions is valuable but greater value for money is achieved across the service because other stakeholders, like the advisory services and the curriculum development service, all know what common infrastructure they can move forward on and can develop their programmes of study, lesson plans and professional support programmes on the basis of a solution that's already in place, particularly with wide-area services. They can put in place quite innovative programmes of teacher support in a very cost-effective way. We can accelerate programmes of change because we know we have an infrastructure that is reliable and on which we can depend.

> 'Teachers' attention is turning to the quality of learning. Children's creativity; the quality and focus of their learning; and their competence in ICT learning are measurably increasing.'

Coherence across the whole Northern Ireland infrastructure has been very valuable. But our focus has been on reliability and availability of the service. We are very keen to make sure that these systems are perceived by schools as being absolutely cast-iron in terms of their ability to deliver curriculum resources into the classroom when the teacher wants them. It's really only now that schools are starting to think about wide-area service. We're looking at this from the perspective of allowing teachers to increasingly personalise the classroom experience for children because the systems will allow the tracking of a child's activities; it will create diagnostic information about a child's performance and a teacher will be able to build their plans for an individual child on the basis of useful information. We are moving into quite a sophisticated e-learning environment which schools will be able to exploit over the next five years. But we need to see improvement in the confidence spreading across the teaching force.

Access for children and teachers from outside is also part of the plan. The wide-area service we've got in place is underpinned by an architecture that provides the 370,000 users of this service with their own unique identity. It doesn't matter whether they come in from a geography classroom or a primary classroom in school or whether they enter through their library or through an Internet service at home, a user will get access to their own unique resource group and be able to access their personal work plans and their homework.

That service is up and running and schools will in many ways be able to break the walls of the classroom down and allow a much more radical way of working with the home.

There isn't a specific parents gateway at the moment or parental routes which are uniquely identified. We currently haven't the service to take on board the 300,000 parents that are out there as well. But that ought to be another step forward. Some schools may want to work with parents and provide them with information. But that's for the future. At the moment parents can come in through the pupil's route. If their son or daughter is online at home the parents can obviously look over their shoulder. We have been exploring some pilot activities to provide information to parents like performance information, but that's in early development at the moment. However, the main gateway for teachers is already there.

We want to continue to develop the service in future. The contract for primary service is about to expire and we're about to refresh that contract, probably with a larger number of computers. We're hoping to move the computer-pupil ratio to one to eight. Our aspiration is one-to-one for the majority of pupils, but, more radically we want to enable the infrastructure so that children can bring in their own devices and, in a secure environment, connect them up such that, although central funding doesn't provide a one-to-one service, the infrastructure that we build is capable of supporting one. We might get to a one to four ratio across the whole estate with school delegated funding contributing as well. The C2K aspiration is create networks that can accommodate 1:1 wireless connectivity. When this is in place the next step is to provide secure access to any mobile device (such as a laptop, tablet, PDA or future generation smart phone) that a teacher or student wants to connect to the network to access its services at any time and anywhere.

2.4

### The future

Over the next five to ten years we can expect to see technology enabling real collegiality, schools working together in partnership, not just with schools, but with other kinds of institutions. The provision of courses will be both face to face and online. School will continue to be very important to provide the social interaction that is at the heart of the educational process. It will be where people go to meet their personal mentors and their friends and to further their personal educational planning and social activities. It will probably help to revalue them, but it won't be where they go predominantly to work because they will be working where they want to work and they will do that where they are comfortable. Where that is doesn't matter, they will be totally mobile, because of the devices that are being developed now.

With our new strategy for the next five years, emPowering Schools, we have set the school service some very ambitious targets to achieve, but wholly necessary if we are to bring the experience of school much closer to the life experience young people have in the 21st century.

# Delivering the vision

**Emile Cubeisy** | Program Director, Jordan Education Initiative, Jordan
**Andreas Cox** | Program Manager, Jordan Education Initiative, Jordan

**The Jordan Education Initiative has as one of its objectives, the improvement of the learning process through public private partnerships, in order to help the government action its vision for education as a catalyst for social and economic development.**

Jordan is a country about the size of Ireland, home to only five million people and – unlike some of our neighbours – with very little natural resources. It is a country that is positioning its sustainability and growth on the quality of its human resources.

It is in that spirit that Jordan has historically invested significant resources into human development, with emphasis on the education and health of its citizens. So while one of the poorer nations in the Middle East, Jordan continuously ranks high in terms of human development indicators when compared to others.

Jordan is a country that is also fast turning the pages of history. King Abdullah II, who succeeded his father King Hussein in 1999, has a vision to initiate and pursue an aggressive strategy of economic and political reform. In the information and communications technology (ICT) sector, this has led to the statutory unbundling of communications monopolies, the funding of ambitious infrastructure programmes, and the implementation of aggressive strategies to attract foreign direct investment. Part of that focus was His Majesty's leadership in the development of an emerging IT sector looking to take advantage of Jordan's qualified human resources.

Couple these initiatives with the fact that over 35 per cent of the population is aged fifteen or younger (compared with only 18–20 per cent in the UK/US) and you can see that Jordan is a country with significant challenges but which also has a clear vision towards the future.

To secure that future, we have to invest in a culture of innovation and launch a new generation of critical thinkers and entrepreneurs. For example, an investment of $100 million in education and infrastructure today could spur just tens of Jordanians to build businesses of the future, but this would create thousands of jobs, export revenue, thus repaying that investment for Jordan.

It is the potential that Jordan holds to be a model country both for the region and beyond that spurred me to get involved. Entrepreneurialism and economic

development were already subjects that I was passionate about. My opportunity came to join the public sector when His Majesty King Abdullah appointed HE Dr Fawaz H Zu'bi to head up the portfolio of Minister of Post and Communications in June 2000. At that time, my experience was in the private sector, where I was contributing to Jordan's vision through the founding and directing of the Young Entrepreneurs Association of Jordan.

I was asked by His Excellency Dr Zu'bi to switch hats and enter the public sector to help manage the inevitable changes that would come about as a result of His Majesty's reforms. As a leader, he empowered me to follow my passion and challenged me to 'think out of the box', thus building in me the confidence aided by strong guidance to drive true innovation. This, tempered with his practical sense for what is achievable, has helped us to adopt an aggressive approach towards achieving the King's vision for Jordan.

2.5

### Getting started

In the early days, it was difficult to identify what I could usefully contribute and what role or roles I could play. I was, however, impassioned by issues arising from connectivity and education. I saw it as incorporating issues related to digital inclusion and overcoming the digital divide. These issues become even more acute when you're dealing with young people – people who have their lives ahead of them and are the real stakeholders in the future that you are creating.

Education became my immediate focus. How do we leverage the fact that we have a captive audience of so many young people in Jordan? How do we create the dynamic changes that the King was and is still looking for today?

As far back as 1999, His Majesty King Abdullah II called on Jordan's IT sector to develop the REACH strategy, a five-year plan focusing on IT development with clear goals for generating new jobs, increasing foreign investment, and generating high-value technology exports. More recently, in 2002 Dr Zu'bi migrated his Ministry of Post and Communications into the more forward-looking Ministry of Information and Communications Technology (MoICT) to articulate and direct the new ICT policies. This Ministry initiated and continues to pursue a programme of significant statutory reform, ranging from the ending of the mobile phone duopoly through to the Government's planned withdrawal from ownership of Jordan Telecom, the establishment of an independent regulator, and engaging in free trade agreements to accelerate the e-economy.

Awareness and access to technology and the Internet slowly began to take off. New initiatives, such as the Knowledge Stations established as community access centres by His Majesty the King, were gaining momentum as catalysts towards the integration of technology into community development. Public universities as well as the Ministry of Education were becoming quick adopters of technology, and an IT curriculum was introduced for all school children.

---

'We wanted to encourage open exploration and discovery as well as strengthen skills of collaborative problem-solving.'

---

Within this context we embarked on the development of a business case for school and university connectivity with the goal of creating a learning eco-system that would bridge schools, community colleges, universities and community access centres to create a knowledge network for the country. It seemed like a logical extension of what was already going on – especially the computerisation of schools (and ADSL connectivity of many), a learning management platform, and two units of the physics curricula which were already being taught electronically – not to mention a number of teacher training programmes as well. Broadband fibre connectivity will provide each school with 100Mbs (and each university with 1Gbs), catalysing school-based innovation, access to applications and digital content, and supporting more efficient deployment and management of school-based technology.

The business case was logical, but people still thought we were crazy. The Government was already planning to invest $380m into educational reform. Now we were proposing a further $80m investment in fibre connectivity. And all this in a country with a per capita GDP of just over $1,700!

The Cabinet, however, saw the logic, as did Parliament. The budget was approved and at the time of writing universities are connected (May 2004) and an RFP has been issued for connecting the first 226 schools.

### The Jordan Education Initiative (JEI)

This initiative was born from real challenges that Jordan had to overcome – both in terms of learning reform and otherwise. How do we align the education offered with the skills required in the new economy? How do we migrate teaching to cater to the way students really learn? How do we infuse the ability for continuous innovation and for teaching students to adapt continuously? We wanted to encourage open exploration and discovery as well as strengthen skills of collaborative problem-solving.

We were fairly confident about the business case proving itself once we had millions of people connected and we had integrated ICT into the classroom. The project was obviously about much more than connectivity however, and it was equally obvious that no one else was doing anything like this, so there were no precedents to learn from. For a country the size of Jordan, we couldn't afford to make mistakes – and it began to dawn on us that if we did this on our own, mistakes would be made.

We wanted to learn how to integrate technology into the learning process and to catalyse cultural change in the classroom. We wanted to make sure that the financial resources invested into learning would develop children into self-supporting citizens.

So the question began to arise: why are we doing this on our own? If this reform was going to build capacity in the labour market for the private sector, and grow market opportunity, why was the private sector not playing an active role in shaping the process and helping us to make the right decisions at the same time?

We therefore made a conscious decision to go out there and see what innovation the private sector had to offer. At this point a golden opportunity presented itself when Cisco Systems' John Chambers stood up in January 2003 at the World Economic Forum [WEF] Annual Meeting and challenged the global CEOs to support educational reform in developing countries. This challenge led to commitments by over 20 WEF participants, commitments that led directly to the foundation of the Jordan Education Initiative.

2.5

It's worth pointing out at this point why I think Jordan was chosen as the pilot country. We may be a small country, but His Majesty has not only articulated a very clear vision of where he wants the country to go, but has also begun vigorously to implement this vision. So you had a receptive government and a population that was very aware of technological change and its potential benefits.

After an extensive scoping phase, the JEI was officially launched in June 2003 at an Extraordinary Meeting of the WEF at the Dead Sea. To launch a project of this size and complexity in only five months is highly unusual, to say the least, but you must remember the initiatives already underway and also – something I think is essential for this sort of operation – active support at a very high level of the executive, in both private and public sectors, including His Majesty King Abdullah II as well as John Chambers, Cisco Systems.

## Enter the global private sector

In the period between the birth of the idea and the official launch of the JEI the WEF member group of IT and telecommunications private sector companies were soul-searching in terms of what contribution they could make. Cisco Systems had already committed to the fast-track development of a maths e-curriculum and other companies were looking to see where their core competence and expertise could make the most positive impact. Computer Associates felt that they could make the most difference in filling a key programme management role to drive and shape the initiative and a phone call on a Friday evening was the hook that brought me into the equation.

Having read the initial brief of the JEI's objectives and coming from a background of managing major change processes, I was naturally sceptical about Jordan's ability to deliver on the bold targets that it had set out for itself. A visit to Jordan and a merry-go-round of visits to a number of e-learning companies as well as the key ministers driving this change left me enthused by the passion and focus of what the country was aiming to achieve. These impressions and Emile's 'can do' attitude left me in no doubt that Jordan was going to deliver on the vision that was the JEI. Within the space of a few days I had bought into this vision – hook, line and sinker!

## Roads to success

In working with the global and local private sector, we identified specific objectives, including the development of a model private–public sector partnership that would improve the development and delivery of education to Jordanian youth. Its focus was on unleashing the innovation of teachers and students while ensuring the sustainability of this model through the development of the capacity of the local information technology industry for the development of innovative learning solutions.

The JEI feeds into two existing national programmes: ERfKE (Education Reform for the Knowledge Economy) and NBLRN (National Broadband Learning and Research Network). The former is a large-scale World Bank supported initiative to raise standards across the board in education, focusing on the curricula, assessment and new methods of learning using ICT. The NBLRN aims to connect all Jordan's educational and community access centres with the objective of linking 1.5 million students by 2006.

Sitting behind these two programmes, the JEI project structure consists of three tracks. The first track targeted 100 Discovery Schools with three integrated initiatives: in-classroom technology (strategies for the introduction of technology that contribute to unleashing teacher and student innovation in a sustainable manner); new e-curricula to drive new learning outcomes; and teacher training to empower teachers not just to feel at ease with but to maximise the utility of our investments.

At the time of writing, the Discovery School project is well on schedule. Activities in all 100 Discovery Schools have been launched, a new maths e-curriculum has been introduced, and is being delivered in 13 schools, and 111 teachers have been trained in the use of the new equipment and the new e-curricula (thanks to partnerships with Cisco Learning Institute, Intel and World Links). To put this into context, the 100 school target will impact over 70,000 students and 2300 teachers.

Private-sector involvement has been enormous. Cisco have provided innovative learning approaches, supported by hardware and software investments. They have also, in association with the Ministry of Education and Rubicon, a local e-learning development company, developed a Grade 1–12 maths e-curriculum, with similar initiatives underway for ICT, Science, Arabic and English sponsored by Microsoft, Fastlink, France Telecom, and the Middle East Partnership Initiative respectively. The local e-learning industry, especially Rubicon, Menhaj, e-Dimensions, and Integrated Technology Solutions, are playing critical roles in the development and delivery of these subjects electronically. Potential partnerships for e-curricula in Civics and Geography are being developed.

---

'The objective of the Lifelong Learning project is to identify the gap between labour market requirements and the skills needed from job-seekers.'

2.5

---

The second and third tracks relate to Lifelong Learning and ICT Industry Development. These are at their early stages. The objective of the Lifelong Learning project is to identify the gap between labour market requirements and the skills needed from job-seekers, and to establish an e-library of knowledge resources available to citizens for bridging the skills gap. To this end, we've set up a partnership between DHL and the Young Entrepreneurs Association of Jordan. They have started with assessing the requirements of Jordanian SMEs, seeing what skills they need to make them more competitive.

The track for ICT Industry Development really arose out of the preparations for JEI itself. In talking with the global private sector during the design phase of the Initiative, it emerged that it was important that their investments also catalysed industry growth, which would lead to sustainability. Tae Yoo, VP for Corporate Philanthropy at Cisco, wanted to ensure that jobs and investments were part of the deliverable aspect of this Initiative, and thus introduced this critical track.

While we were working with local companies to determine possible partners for developing the new e-curricula, we came into daily contact with management and with them began to see ways in which the project itself could introduce new skill-sets and further improve our IT industry knowledge base. This area of the project is now being led by INTAJ (the Information Technology Association of Jordan) under the guidance of Amish Mehta at CommercialWare/Corel.

Perhaps the scale of this project is becoming apparent. We now have over 45 partners, ranging from non-profit organisations like the Krach Family Foundation NetCorps and World Links, through to government departments and multinational corporations like Cisco Systems, HP, Microsoft, France Telecom, IBM, Dell, Computer Associates and Intel.

### Managing the JEI: a challenge in itself

Front-line management is carried out by the Program Management Office (PMO) which is based in Jordan, has full-time staff, and carries overall responsibility for the project. The design of the PMO is a challenge in itself, as we are introducing global skill sets in management to a Jordanian team that will carry forward the mandate of the Initiative. Global partners have been leading this effort in upgrading the skills of Jordanian management in the implementation of such large-scale projects. Sitting behind the PMO are the Academic Advisory Board, the Executive Steering Committee, and the Stakeholder Committee. In this way, the interests of learning, corporate investment and private/public/administrative parties are all protected.

### Challenges and achievements

In terms of converting the vision into operational practice, we have learnt several valuable lessons which we would like to share.

---

'Syria, Bahrain, Iraq, Kuwait and Saudi Arabia have all witnessed the potential success of the JEI model and have expressed interest in leveraging our acquired knowledge and experience.'

---

The first problem we had was quite simple: how do we sell the JEI concept to partners? We needed to get them to think differently about how they approached their engagement in education – a question often complicated by the fact that many countries themselves don't have a clear vision of where they're going in this area. For the companies involved, it requires a change of mind-set, a shifting of vision from their normal business focus to more of a sustainable development approach.

One of the key issues here is what we can only call 'short-termism'. The value of a project like this is not realised in weeks or even months – it's realised over many years. Companies would come to the project with preconceptions about what they could immediately deliver or receive, in either technological or business terms. We had to introduce a new focus on innovation and development, asking not how we get an immediate return, but how we find the right answers to some very difficult long-term issues. We are a process that is transferring knowledge and capacity for educational innovation, not solutions in boxes. Once that's done, the environment we would create would generate business opportunities for the future. In a nutshell, convincing people to look three years and not three months ahead was our biggest challenge.

The answer to wooing private partners is to convince them of the benefit. When initially presented, people were asking, 'How many computers do we provide? How many laptops? Projectors?' But our real need – as we said earlier – was not the hardware. We could buy that. What we needed was exposure to innovative practice and knowhow and, most important, that was also what we had to offer. We knew that our global partners would learn from engaging in this process – about how to interact with developing countries, how to build solutions outside their backyard, solutions that could work in many markets – as we would learn from them. This is already happening: Syria, Bahrain, Iraq, Kuwait and Saudi Arabia have all witnessed the potential success of the JEI model and have expressed interest in leveraging our acquired knowledge and experience.

The next big challenge involved integrating the project with Jordan's existing educational strategy. How would we add value to what was already being done? This project initially arrived at the Ministry of Information and Communications Technology before it arrived at the Ministry of Education and we could have taken that lead and turned it – reduced it, we should say – to a mere technological initiative. So we had to place ourselves in the position of servant, not of master. What was our niche? How could we add value to an educational reform process that was already underway? You can't start derailing existing and very successful national initiatives unless you can prove that you are really going to add value.

2.5

It is here where the leadership of HE Dr Khaled Toukan, our Minister of Education, has been phenomenal. He continues to be able to shape and drive the programmes of the Initiative to realise maximum potential in the delivery of Jordan's broader education goals. He has enabled the initiative to focus on innovation, and to feed back the learnings into other facets of the reform process. The balance at times is delicate, but he has positioned the initiative as a change agent to catalyse far-reaching education reform.

Our next word of warning is a familiar one, but none the less important for that. It's about managing people's expectations. You've got corporate partners, the Ministry of Education, school administrators, teachers, students and even parents all looking to you to deliver. A project like this is for the long term, but people are often looking for immediate change. A teacher who's waiting for a laptop has a very different perspective from a group trying to formulate strategy for best practice in ICT.

Project management has been an enormous challenge, naturally. The public sector has a lot to learn from industry about management, accurate assessment, business case analysis and how to deploy these techniques. We think that we're not really there yet – a lot of what we do is still quite ad-hoc. Sometimes that arises from one of the JEI's strengths – that it's both a grass-roots as well as a top-down initiative. But it's not as process-oriented as we would have liked it to be. We actually thought it would be different: that we'd have lots of management structure in place before we started implementation but – as we'll point out in a moment – that hasn't been the case. It turns out that the management of innovation within corporate as well as public sector structures involving over 45 partners has required different skill sets than those normally demanded by conventional project management philosophies. We are convinced that a key secret to the success in what has been achieved to date has been the flexibility for involvement and innovation that we have allowed in the process – a factor which would normally kill any complex project process. The initiative is now fuelled by informal networks that transcend company name and cross into the individual passion of visionaries in global and local entities. What's more exciting is that many are carrying that spirit back into their own corporations.

Our final point is about establishing a cohesive identity for the project. We still don't have a common JEI culture. The project needs to communicate a clear image of what it is and where it's going, so that partners can identify more easily how they can contribute. The support of the government ministers and the global CEOs has been tremendous and we're sure it will carry us through the teething process as we convert the enthusiasm into a clearly identified single vision and an organic, functional process.

Three things that counter the challenges above have astonished us about this initiative. First, we could not possibly have hoped for so many partners to become involved and for them all to work together so cooperatively and selflessly. The World Economic Forum has been exemplary in building support for the Initiative, and in helping us reach out across the world to identify corporations with a will for change. Companies are – understandably – very reserved, guarded and protective about how they communicate, but JEI and the WEF have created a very positive environment, with companies talking to schools, government departments, teachers, students and each other.

Secondly, we simply never imagined that we would have achieved so much at this stage – less than twelve months into the project. We've got a curriculum up and running, wireless in the schools, laptops and projectors in the classrooms and trained (and excited) teachers.

For the PMO, a key third and unexpected success has been the Ministry of Education's enthusiasm and support for the effort. The mobilisation that has taken place to allow for deployment of the Maths e-curriculum, as an example, has been tremendous. Incident-filled, yes, but you feel capacity developing on a daily basis.

The biggest lesson we've learned is that it's possible. You *can* get the private sector (both here and abroad), the government, the World Economic Forum, the head teachers, the students – everyone – throwing their weight wholeheartedly behind a single programme.

### Looking ahead

The Discovery Schools are now up and running. So where will we be in two years' time? The JEI has shown us that you can break down the walls surrounding every classroom and open it up to the world outside. It has given us a vision of an entirely new type of classroom, where students can interact with the world around them.

---

'We've got a curriculum up and running, wireless in the schools, laptops and projectors in the classrooms and trained (and excited) teachers.'

---

All of us are born in very different circumstances and it would be presumptuous to say that every Jordanian will one day be able to see, touch and feel the world. The openness of ICT is enabling students to break down their preconceptions of reality, and empowering them to build their own horizons, their own futures.

2.5

By putting students more in charge of their own education, I think we'll see increasing differentiation between classrooms. The students will play a greater role in defining their environment and learning experience. Brighter students can move ahead more easily; those with challenges will receive more support and opportunity, more personalised learning. This is going to lead to a cultural, social revolution, the boundaries of which none of us can predict today.

It's not just students, either. Teachers will have a much more enlightened role in the future. They will no longer be instruments of the curriculum, but truly have the potential to master it. They will innovate much more effectively in the classroom, responding to their own sense of what the students need. They will go beyond the books, challenging students to research and learn about what motivates them and – crucially – about what is relevant today, not three years ago or whenever the textbooks were written. As teacher capacities develop, early adopters will inspire more and more of their peers to leverage a new school environment to stimulate students in the way they really learn.

As a result, we hope to see teachers redefining for themselves their role in the classroom. The JEI is giving them the resources, knowledge and opportunity to do that.

We see students empowered to set their own learning agenda in these new classrooms without walls, having a more active role in their homes, their communities and their country. As a result – and paradoxically – the real knowledge transfer here may well not be into the classroom, but out of it. If that happens at the local level, it will be mirrored at the national level: a steady flow of conscious learning and understanding out into the world.

JEI will accelerate the process of Jordan's leapfrogging stages of development, and can – and most probably will – be implemented elsewhere. Lessons from this initiative will help others build, shape, share and adapt their visions for education into continuous cycles of innovation. The whole world can be part of that. Moore's law told us that processing power will double every eighteen months. Our hope is that the JEI will lead to a similar phenomenon in the sharing and propagation of educational development for the benefit of generations to come.

None of this would have been possible, however, without the JEI team, who daily live the vision of the JEI. Thanks, team!

# Policy frameworks

# Education and ICT: the potential for personalisation

**David Miliband** | Minister of State for School Standards, Department for Education and Skills, England.

**David Miliband explores two great challenges: the challenge of equity and excellence; and the challenge of universality and personalisation.**

Education and modern technology are a powerful combination. Together they hold the potential to deepen economic prosperity and tackle inequalities in society by engaging more citizens in their own learning. In the UK, it is an exciting time for their alliance – our independent tests and international studies tell us that standards in our schools are rising; and that on average they are rising fastest in our most disadvantaged areas.

• Our independent inspectorate, the Office for Standards in Education (Ofsted) tell us that we have the best generation of teachers and teacher trainees ever,

• The proportion of teachers with the confidence to use ICT in their subject teaching increased from about 6 in 10 in 1998 to almost 9 in 10 last year,

• Our students have better access to the benefits of ICT with 99 per cent of schools now connected to the internet, and with the number of pupils per computers used for teaching and learning down from over 17 in primary schools in 1998 to less than 8 in 2003; and down from over 8 in secondary schools to just above 5 now.

So there is much to celebrate. But there is also a lot still to achieve. Whilst the proportion of our 16 year olds achieving five good GCSEs has increased from 45 per cent in 1997 to 53 per cent in 2003, this is still almost half our young people not gaining the passport they need into work and adult life. We also do not do well enough at encouraging young people to stay on in education after the age of 16. The UK came 24th out of 29 OECD countries for post-16 participation. The top country Sweden has 98 per cent involved in education or training. In the UK it is only 74 per cent. In an increasingly knowledge driven economy, where an estimated 9 out of 10 new jobs demands high standards in ICT, numeracy and literacy, we can ill afford such a massive waste of talent.

## Two great challenges

Our goal is to help every leaner fulfil their potential. Standing in the way are two great challenges: the challenge of equity and excellence; and the challenge of universality and personalisation.

We see the challenge of excellence and equity in many debates. In an unequal society, how can excellent provision serve the least fortunate, rather than the most? One answer is to say it cannot; excellence will always be monopolised by the well-off, so we should simply tackle poor performance.

3.1

I believe this is profoundly wrong. We must obviously tackle failure. But aside from the absurdity of trying to put a glass ceiling on the achievement of different services, excellence can be used as a battering ram against inequality. This is the experience of specialist schools and the Excellence in Cities and Leading Edge programmes in education. They have demonstrated that excellence is a resource for a more egalitarian system, not a threat. Excellence can do more than set an example; it can be a locomotive for improvement across the system.

The second challenge is the demand that universal services have a personal focus. Some people argue that by definition mass services cannot deliver the personal touch. I disagree. Services for all citizens can be customised to the needs of each citizen. In education we call it personalised learning. It means building the organisation of schooling around the needs, interests and aptitudes of individual pupils; it means shaping teaching around the way different youngsters learn; and it means taking the care to nurture the unique talents of every pupil.

I believe personalised learning is the debate in education today. It is the way to tackle disadvantage and ensure every leaner fulfils their potential. In this essay I want to set out what are in my view its five key elements. I want to demonstrate how ICT is central to each. And I want to discuss the challenge of delivering personalised learning for every child.

### Personalised learning

Personalised learning is the way in which our best schools tailor education to ensure that every pupil achieves the highest standard possible. Our drive is to make these best practices universal. There are five key elements to doing so.

### Assessment for learning

First, a personalised offer in education depends on really knowing the strengths and weaknesses of individual students. So the biggest driver for change is assessment for learning and the use of data and dialogue to diagnose every student's learning needs.

Too often in the past hunches about performance have distracted from clear evidence about what will drive up individual attainment. Some pupils have been allowed to coast at their own preferred pace, rather than being helped along as fast as they can.

---

'A one size fits all approach to education puts brakes on the progress of too many students.'

---

Personalised learning demands instead hard facts not soft assumptions about pupil achievement, benchmarked against national standards. At Seven Kings School in Redbridge the combination of student tracking and agreed individual targets has helped tackle underperformance right across the school. The result: overall attainment up from about half of students achieving 5 good GCSEs in 1997 to over three-quarters last year. Embed these practices in all schools and we will achieve a step-change in achievement.

ICT supports this ambition. For teachers, it offers effective tracking of individual progress by combining instant feedback with the opportunity to identify trends in learning. That is why the national Pupil Achievement Tracker is now at the heart of our drive to ensure critical self review of performance in every school. For students, ICT offers the development of an e-portfolio to record their challenges, experiences, revisions and successes. This supports high-quality feedback, reflective learning, self esteem, and a deeper understanding for parents about their child's learning.

### Teaching for learning

Second, personalised learning demands that teachers actively engage all students and accommodate their different styles of learning. No easy task. And a challenge that demands innovation.

A striking feature in parts of our culture is the endurance of a century-old model of passive knowledge absorption. This is the presumption that teachers should speak and the class should remain silent. An effective model for some learning tasks, and a real achievement with some learning groups! But a one size fits all approach to education puts brakes on the progress of too many students.

To help all fulfil their potential, teaching strategies must engage and stretch all students. This is the thinking behind putting better pay and professional development to the service of meeting student needs. We want every teacher to be motivated to identify their own development goals, whether that be to overcome barriers to learning, to develop the use of ICT in their own subject specialisms, or to extend learning opportunities through for example tailored programmes for particularly gifted and talented students.

It is also the thinking behind our drive for more and better use of ICT in the classroom. Interactive whiteboards have provided a first step. They help students understand more complex concepts[1] and they help teachers use web and network-based resources to support learning.[2] The Department for Education and Skills has invested £50 million over the past two years to make this new technology a reality for more and more students.

But the impact of ICT can go even further. It can encourage more active student participation. At Kemnal Technology College in Kent for example online group work is regularly used to stimulate classroom discussion. The result: from about 80 per cent of students saying that they felt unwilling or apprehensive about contributing in class, down to just 15 per cent now in online lessons; and teachers reporting that student contribution has improved in the traditional classrooms as well.

E-learning fits well with the culture of today's learners. Yet Ofsted tell us that only two in ten schools make effective use of new technologies within the curriculum. The challenge is to integrate ICT into the wider learning experience, to help all pupils build confidence in their learning, to unleash their creativity and motivation, and to help fulfil their potential.

## Curriculum choice

Third, personalised learning demands a curriculum choice that engages and respects students, with clear pathways through the system. In other words choice within school as well as choice between school. In primary schools, it means students gaining high standards in the basics allied to opportunities for enrichment and creativity. In the early secondary years, it means students actively engaged by exciting curricula, problem-solving, and class participation. And then at 14-19, it means significant curriculum choice for the learner.

New GCSEs in subjects such as ICT, engineering, health and social care are a new and important way to combine broader choice with more intellectual stretch. For the longer term, the Tomlinson working group on 14-19 education has the goal of providing for all students incentives to learn, core skills and specialist vocational and academic options. It is a future already being charted by diverse groups of schools, colleges and employers across the country. ICT is at the forefront of delivery, such as:

- Knowles Hill school in Devon, where healthcare students benefit from a video conferencing link with Bromangymnaiset school in Hudiksvall Sweden. The students take one topic each week and investigate the facilities available in their two communities. These discussions serve as a basis for written work which is credited towards their final qualification.

- The schools in Nottingham that are working with engineers from UK One Racing to map the design and technology skills employed in making a mini motorbike to the Engineering GCSE. This will form part of a regional Minimoto championship, supported by a website designed by students in their ICT and Art and Design GCSE programmes.

1. Smith, H. (2001)
Smart board Evaluation, Kent Ngfl
www.kented.org.UK/ngfl/
whitespends/report.html

2. Walker, D. (2003)
Quality at the Dockside,
TES online, 3 January 2003,
pp. 66–67

3.1

E-learning provides a means of tailoring curriculum choice to the needs of students at all levels of study and ability. It gives teachers greater scope to provide flexible learning programmes. And it makes it easier for students to go further and faster in the areas that interest them most.

### Radical approach to school organisation

Fourth, personalised learning demands a student-centred approach to school organisation. This means schools creating an ethos of high standards and high expectations for all. It means students involved in the drive for whole school improvement. And it means staff having the time, support and skills necessary to give every pupil the attention they desire.

Workforce remodelling is absolutely key. Our national agreement on workforce reform is designed to give teachers more time to prepare and plan lessons, and more and better support from a flexible whole school team – made up not only of teachers and head teachers, but teaching assistants, learning mentors and behavioural support staff – a vital means of responding to individual need and raising standards.

Building on these insights, we also want schools to make the most of their many other resources. I call this the productivity challenge for school leaders, as it demands that they think creatively about how best to support high-quality teaching and learning.

ICT is an opportunity for real progress. It offers the means to less duplication by enabling teachers to prepare lesson plans, worksheets and reports as a network resource. It enables the more efficient delegation of tasks to support staff. Its effective use can free-up time for a teacher to teach of between 3.25 and 4.55 hours every week.[3]

3. PriceWaterhouseCoopers (2001) Teacher Workload Study: Final Report. London: DfES

ICT can also help radically change the way schools work. Their four walls are no longer a constraint to pupil progress. ICT allows schools to be open 24 hours a day, 7 days a week. A vision that is already becoming a reality at Lynn Grove High School in Norfolk. Its 'Virtual School' is used extensively out of hours, with many students spending longer periods of time on homework because they find the online materials and support provide a more satisfying learning experience to studying alone.

### Strong local partnerships

Fifth, personalised learning means parents, the community, local institutions and social services supporting schools to drive forward progress in the classroom. There is already real innovation in using ICT to make this happen:

• To build a stronger partnership with parents. Shireland Language College in Sandwell is working with its six primary school partners to use ICT to provide parents with more and better information about their children's progress. Every family has been given a computer on loan, and parents have been trained to view their children's homework online.

## A laptop learning culture at
## Ninestiles Schools and Technology College

Nearly 1,000 laptops are in use at Ninestiles. Every member of staff has one. So do most of the pupils. It means that learning can take place wherever they are, at any time of the day and at any time in the week, including during holidays. 'It's a major reason for the school having improved so dramatically,' says Cathy Holland, assistant head teacher who manages the 'Anytime anywhere learning' programme for the school. The proportion of students achieving 5 good GCSEs has increased from just 35 per cent in 2000 up to 75 per cent last year.

The laptop scheme began in March 2000, when only 15 members of staff had laptops. Now a subsidised scheme with Toshiba enables students to lease a laptop for £8 per week over three years. Students entitled to free school meals may have one for £5 per week. And each faculty has a bank of laptops for use in school by students who do not hire their own.

Ninestiles also has a campus-wide wireless network – one of the largest educational networks in Europe. This allows instant Internet and server access for teachers and pupils; meaning pupils can do research, view webcams, get involved in videoconferencing within Britain or overseas, and have access to interactive learning sites filtered by the school.

Educationally, the school identifies several key benefits of its laptop culture. For students: increased confidence and creativity; broadened thinking skills; independent learning; and progress towards real life workplace skills. For staff: enhanced continuous development; greater integration of ICT into the curriculum; and an increasing scope of educational resources. For parents: the opportunity to engage in their child's learning at home; and a real resource for the whole family.

The widespread use of ICT contributes to what one student described as 'the strong work ethic' at Ninestiles: 'We're encouraged to work hard and do well, partly because we can learn anywhere, and learning is at the centre of everything the school does. Laptops make education more flexible,' she said.

Source: Specialist Schools Trust 2004

The next stage of the project will enable parents to access their children's achievement and attendance data so that they can work with schools to identify and respond to each child's individual learning needs.

- To improve attendance and behaviour. Ratton School in East Sussex has established a Parents Gateway. Parents can log-on to the school network from home and work to access information about their child. Details on attendance are automatically updated every morning so parents concerned about truanting can check up on whether their child is in attendance.

- To integrate services at the school, Millfields Community school in Hackney has developed a wide range of extended provision. Its offer to students includes a breakfast club that opens at 7am, play centre provision until 6pm, and a Saturday school that teaches an accelerated learning curriculum for Key Stage 2 pupils. The school is also proactive in educating parents on how best to support their children, providing guidance on the educational system and the curriculum, as well as family learning courses in literacy, numeracy and ICT.

The red thread running through the five elements of personalised learning is the tailoring of provision to meet the needs and develops the talents of all students. ICT holds a special capacity to drive this forward. The challenge is to ensure that all students benefit from both.

### The challenge of delivery

The old model of delivery would have followed the 'idea – legislation – implementation' process; a model at the heart of the 1944 Education Act, which saw education as 'a national system… to be local-administered'. Yet this produced a regulatory culture that is out of touch with the way local professionals want to develop their schools. The challenge for government is to build capacity in local systems by providing national leadership and support. There are four central aspects of this role that demand attention.

'Partnerships between school, colleges, higher education and business are also important, putting a wider pool of skills at the service of young people.'

First, there is no substitute for schools leading reform. Professional collaboration and networking help to generate excellence. Our goal is to enable our best schools to become locomotives of progress in others; with our best teachers helping the rest; and our best departments sharing their best practice. The hard edge of this collaboration is improvement, with schools developing the capacity to deliver personalised learning. That is the purpose of:

- The 4,000-strong network of Advanced Skill Teachers, with 316 focussing specifically on ICT, who spend the equivalent of one day a week helping other teachers outside their own school improve their offer.

- The Leading Edge Programme, in which 100 schools work with 600 partners to tackle some of our toughest learning challenges – including efforts to increase achievement amongst pupils from disadvantaged and/or minority ethnic backgrounds.

- The Excellence in Cities programme, that develops school partnerships and shared responsibility for, amongst other things, opportunities for gifted and talented students, Learning Mentors, and City Learning Centres that give pupils better access to the latest education technology.

- The online communities of professionals, who are debating reform, discussing what works in their own classrooms, and helping to chart the future of education.

3.1

Second, there is no substitute for sponsored innovation. That is the evidence of our new Academies programme. Academies are independent schools in the state sector, licensed by the Secretary of State, and directed at areas of economic poverty and educational underachievement. They demonstrate that radical innovation can transform the structure and culture of schools beset by endemic underperformance. They do things differently to raise attainment: like a five term year, an extended day, longer learning sessions, better use of ICT, a bigger role for governors.

Sponsored innovation is also vital in a variety of other ways. The National College of School Leadership helps head teachers innovate so as to make the most of their resources – by engaging students as co-producers in education, by thinking strategically about how to deploy their staff, and by using networked ICT resources to support more effective management. Innovative partnerships between school, colleges, higher education and business are also important, putting a wider pool of skills at the service of young people. Our national partnership with Cisco is broadening their opportunities to engage with new technology. There are now 620 Cisco Networking Academies that reach about 24,000 students across the country.

Third, there is no substitute for realising the full potential of every professional. This is the importance of what I call an informed professionalism, one in which the whole school team gains the capability and flexibility to drive forward the achievement of students. The challenge is how we combine this flexibility in delivery with accountability for results. I believe the answer must be intelligent accountability: a system that both supports improvement and challenges the lack of it. That is why we are developing a new relationship with schools. To give them the benefits of:

- Just one single conversation with all national partners about their targets, priorities and support, with just one plan providing the basis for all funding.
- Shorter, sharper inspection which helps prioritise action for improvement.
- A relationship with parents based on a clear and shared understanding of school priorities and progress.
- A communication system that uses the capacity of the internet to deliver to heads and teachers the information that they need, when they need it and in the form in which they need it.

Fourth, there is no substitute to high standards for every student. That is the moral purpose of education: every young person having the right to fulfil their potential. To do so they need to benefit from high expectations and high aspirations.

Objective, national benchmarks of achievement are vital. They give students, parents and teachers clear feedback and a challenge where necessary to underachievement. That is the moral as well as educational case for tests and appropriate targets. It is why the answer to the limitations of league tables is more information not less. It is why we are using the power of ICT to supplement raw achievement scores with value-added data.

Investment to match reform is also vital. I am proud to be part of a Government that has made an historic commitment to the education system, raising education spending as a share of national income from 4.7 per cent in 1996/97 to 5.6 per cent in 2007/08. This is investment to ensure a step change in provision. It is investment to ensure ICT helps drive up attainment. In 1998, the first year of the National Grid for Learning, the Government invested £102m in ICT for schools. In 2006 it will invest over £700m.

## Conclusion

ICT holds the potential to drive forward a revolution in English education. I believe it can help build a universal education system tailored to the needs and talents of individual students.

This demands changes in the structure of our schooling system. High standards for every student. The informed and supported professionalism of every teacher. A centre of excellence in every school. And networks of collaboration that achieve and sustain improvement.

It also demands a change in culture. New technology can be a frightening prospect; something for tomorrow; the pursuit of the next generation. Yet success demands that we harness the potential of ICT now, to achieve effectiveness and efficiency goals.

That means a critical mass of schools using networked ICT resources, because the best gains are achieved when everyone is engaged, not through isolated developments. It means ICT embedded in teaching and learning so that students benefit in the classroom. And it means collaboration between connected schools, colleges, universities and employers learning from each other and helping each other to lead reform.

The evidence is that this is possible. I look forward to working with all our partners in education to make it a reality.

3.1

# France's vision of the school of the future

**François Fillon** I Minister of Education, France

**François Fillon discusses France's vision of the school of the future, its national e-education strategy, and how it will be achieved.**

### The digital school of tomorrow

The school of tomorrow will be a multimedia school, where all pupils will have the same access to resources wherever they live and whatever their socio-economic situation. It will be a school that knows how to use new technologies to deliver social integration.

Every school will have a web portal where the pupils, teachers and teaching staff will have the opportunity to meet and share information. This virtual space will include personalised sections that will be perfectly secure. The school will have video-conference facilities that will allow communication between schools and provide a bridge to the wider world. Teaching will be delivered in an exciting multimedia manner through lesson plans illustrated with written and audiovisual material. Supported by a broadband infrastructure, which will cover the whole school, downloading of documents will be as simple as a click and will of course take only a matter of seconds.

Pupils will be used to dealing with a rich content that they will exploit with ease. They will know how to make the best use of this content without being taken in by imprecise, prejudiced or ill-founded information; their teachers will have taught them how to learn, will have developed their critical faculties in relation to information sources and will have encouraged a good understanding of their civic rights and duties and a respect for ethics on the Net. These children will understand the codes of good practice in the information society and will respect them. Robust arrangements will protect them from material that is inappropriate for minors and will ensure that they have a confident and secure Internet experience.

In short, the digital school that we want for tomorrow will be integrated into its local and international environment and open to the world, its history, geography, cultures and people. It will be a school that facilitates dialogue between the generations, cultures and pupils themselves.

## Measures undertaken by the French government to realise this vision

France has a comprehensive plan for the development of new technologies – PLAN RESO 2007 – covering all ministries. Schools play a key role in three chapters of the plan strongly supported by all government members:

1 Developing an understanding of, and the ability to use, information and communication technology (ICT);

3.2

2 Support for the development of multimedia educational material that meets pedagogical needs and promotion of its use;

3 Encouraging hardware provision and infrastructure development.

## Developing access to multimedia content and reducing the digital divide

To respond to the urgent challenge of promoting digital literacy the Ministry of Education and the Delegation for Internet Usage have adopted a proactive strategy of promoting access to and use of the Internet by young people, families and the wider public.

Providing free public Internet access points is a key part of the strategy. The public strategy has brought all such points together under the 'NetPublic' brand and declared them a resource for the whole public. Public sponsors want these to be pleasant places, culturally and geographically close to the citizen. They should be part of everyday life, the local institution that actively encourages the kind of Internet usage that has a strong added social value. These public Internet access points are supported in a number of specific ways:

• By offering a number of ICT training programmes: for example, the 'Internet and Multimedia Passport', aimed at the general public who want to polish up their skills and be given some form of recognition for their Internet abilities. Distance learning courses are also offered, which will provide a diploma to staff of the NetPublic access points and ensure they can support the public as effectively as possible. The Ministry of Education is currently piloting this programme and plans to make it generally available in the near future.

• By offering financial benefits: our private sector partners have agreed to extend financial support for these sites, that was in principle negotiated exclusively for schools, enabling them to have access to services and content (in particular, in relation to authors' rights) on better terms.

• By encouraging access to the most disadvantaged: from September 2004 a programme of support will be in place for economically disadvantaged individuals who will be able to seek assistance from NetPublic staff in navigating public sector websites (eg employment, health, housing). In this way they will be taken care of more directly and be shown how to make the most of e-administration procedures in a way that will cater for their immediate practical needs.

By promoting a balanced discussion of the Internet: our citizens need to discover the benefits of the Internet, but it is also important to alert them to certain dangers and remind them of the basic rules of civility and republican justice to which France remains attached. The Internet should not be used to steal the intellectual property of others, in particular, music; or to bombard people with emails they do not want. Sources of information should be checked and respect should be given to those with whom you are in dialogue, even if you can't see them.

### Development of content

The digital school is not just about electronic teaching material, but also recognises that e-enablement is not the be-all and end-all. The Web is a tool to improve the life of the school in all its aspects, pedagogical and administrative, but is not a substitute for the other elements that make a good school.

'Pupils, teachers and parents will have easy access to a comprehensive range of tools, services and content: pupils will have a real "electronic schoolbag".'

In relation to content the ministry is working on two complementary pilot projects with the aim of subsequently making them generally available. The first is the digital workspace whose basic idea is very simple: using new technologies every pupil, teacher and parent should be able to get easier access to information about school life and have a web portal to fulfil this function. The ministry's project provides a basic infrastructure which can be added to and completed as necessary. Pupils, teachers and parents will have easy access to a comprehensive range of tools, services and content: pupils will have a real 'electronic schoolbag' containing their lessons, homework as well as timetable; teachers will be able to consult the files of individual pupils, create workgroups according to ability; parents will be able to follow the academic progress of their children much better by accessing test results and school reports, enabling them to have improved dialogue with teachers and the school administration. One of the big innovations of this project will be to make this whole environment remotely accessible from any place inside or outside school and regardless of the means and type of Internet access.

This implies using technical solutions that are as open as possible, in particular, solutions supporting the provision of new services to meet the needs of mobile users. Culturally this has to be recognised as a revolution of great symbolic importance, when you contrast this with the current operation of the school that is physically highly concentrated.

The project has a special focus on people with disabilities – technical solutions have been developed for their benefit (whether it is a matter of physical, audio-visual or cognitive disabilities).

A personal information and workspace will be available for every pupil, teacher and parent by 2007.

The second initiative is the 'Digital knowledge space' programme. This is a portal containing all kinds of general information, statistics and material on literary and general culture that will be accessible to schools and where the Ministry has negotiated a right to use from the publishers. The aim here is of course complementary to the digital work space project with the fundamental difference that the digital knowledge space will only be accessible from schools both for pedagogical and intellectual copyright reasons.

3.2

The aim of the Ministry in regard to this project is not just pedagogical. We also want to encourage this important economic sector by creating new outlets for the production of digital content. If these tools are successful in the classrooms, publishers will follow suit. They may even seek to refine their market studies and satisfy the expectations of the public in a virtuous circle where demand encourages supply. Sometimes we see the opposite. We all know very well that certain subjects are better served in terms of digital content than others. If the digital knowledge space gives the same space to all the subjects taught in school, it will perhaps create a dynamic for subjects that are perhaps left behind today, making them economically a little more attractive and encouraging publishers to take more of an interest in them.

As far as content is concerned, we are committed to guaranteeing pupils risk-free access to the Internet. This commitment underlines all the projects. Giving pupils free access to the Internet is a great responsibility in relation to families and you need to know what you are doing. France has taken several initiatives in this area. In relation to families, public authorities have sought to build awareness and understanding to protect children who use the Internet. They have also taken specific steps in relation to the pupils themselves. The ministry itself continues to recommend to the general public tools facilitating safe navigation of the Net. A series of concrete measures have been approved by the Consultative Internet Council which was set up in February 2004. For example, the creation of www.mineurs.fr site has been announced, which permits people to highlight illicit sites and inform families of their rights. The publication and dissemination of a comparative study of filtering software is on the same lines. Overall, the Ministry has adopted a strategy of formulating and encouraging codes of behaviour that constitute a responsible use of the Net adapted to the needs of the education system.

Following the work of the World Information Society Summit, French authorities are working with their international counterparts to develop an international code of morality and common courtesy in relation to use of the Net.

## Hardware provision and infrastructure development

The French government plan envisages one computer for every ten school pupils by 2007 and one computer for every three pupils in lycees and colleges. This is a significant budgetary effort but reflects the level of political commitment.

This will not be sufficient, of course. It is also necessary to encourage computer penetration and Internet usage in the family itself. Undoubtedly the most popular measure we have taken in this area is the agreement reached by the state in November 2003 with the main computer manufacturers to provide computers to the general public at preferential prices. A campaign was undertaken with the label 'Internet declared a public utility' in December 2003. A third of computers sold in the Christmas period were sold on this basis. Since the start of 2004, the industry has seen a sharp increase in the sale of computers, proving this initiative worked. The ministry is using this approach again in 2004 but targeted at more specific sectors of the population – students, old people, parents of school children, people looking for work.

Within the context of this campaign the Ministry has put together a special offer for students for laptop computers with wireless access to the Internet. The agreement negotiated with the manufacturers provides preferential prices for equipment, content and services. It is also putting in place a simplified payment plan (one euro per day per student) as well as free subscription to broadband on university campuses.

Alternative technologies (WiFi, Wi-Max etc.) are also strongly supported because they help reduce the digital divide and allow mobile Internet access. France is currently number three in the world in terms of density of coverage with more than 2000 WiFi hotspots. Deployment of wireless net infrastructure is strongly encouraged and due to strong public private partnerships, the development of this type of infrastructure has been accelerated in France. For examples, ten NetPublic public Internet access points are WiFi-enabled and the aim is to enable a hundred in the next twelve months; more and more large hospitals are becoming Wi-Fi-enabled – Necker, Trousseau, Robert Debré and Dijon; 50 per cent of universities are enabled and we want to encourage schools, colleges and lycées in this direction (so far only 80 schools and a few dozen colleges and lycées are WiFi-enabled, but it's a start!).

These first large-scale experiments by the Delegation for Use of the Internet enable the development of broadband Internet access and promote awareness of it. They will be followed by other national and local initiatives to test the economic and social relevance of broadband and its concrete impact on e-enablement of the country.

### The teaching profession as key actor in e-school transformations

France's education community is on the way and making good progress – this is proved by the fact that teachers are participating in these developments even if at times everybody admits it can be difficult for them.

---

'The political objective behind this initiative is simple: to give each future citizen training in long-term use of ICT.'

---

3.2

In France, it has been decided to begin by making ICT training compulsory in schools, which seems a good way of ensuring that new technologies are brought into schools. The IT and Internet Certificate (B2i) was made compulsory in secondary schools last year for the pupils in year three (on average 15 years old). The political objective behind this initiative is simple: to give each future citizen training in long-term use of ICT – in some cases for future development as ICT professionals. The paradox which nobody in the Ministry will hide is that while pupils sit their B2i certificates at the end of year three not all teachers are in a position to prepare them for these certificates. This is a risk that public authorities have consciously taken. But at the end of the day progress is needed and what better way to encourage teachers than to focus the energies of their pupils on these subjects.

Today only 20 per cent of primary and secondary teachers in France use multimedia materials in their lessons. This is too few and represents an enormous challenge for us. We need to make sure we have the means to meet this challenge.

The first point to make is that France currently has a unique demographic opportunity that we must seize – 40 per cent of the teaching profession in primary and secondary schools will change between now and 2010 due to planned retirement. It makes sense therefore to speed up the training of the young teachers who will take up the baton. With this aim in mind we have set up an IT and Internet certificate (C2i) in the teacher training institutions beginning in autumn 2004 and of course we are undertaking a wider awareness-building programme.

To sum up, I am very confident that our teachers will give very active support to our young pupils as they learn not just the benefits of these new tools but also how to tame or domesticate them. Our aim is to enable our young citizens to become enlightened adults in their use of new technologies.

# Technology for knowledge's sake

**Lyle Oberg** | Minister Of Learning, Alberta, Canada

**Under Dr Oberg's leadership, Alberta's learning system has evolved into a more integrated education system with stronger links between the grade-school and post-secondary sectors. As Minister, he has highlighted the importance of lifelong learning and worked tirelessly to create a system that supports individuals in this ongoing pursuit. Dr Oberg also supports a learning system that is flexible and responsive. His focus on continuous improvement is directed at both the learning system and the learner, and he believes strongly in collaboration between government and stakeholders.**

One of the primary goals in Alberta is to produce better citizens. Someone leaving the school system with vast amounts of knowledge, but few social or citizenship skills is not necessarily a good functioning member of society. Knowledge together with citizenship is extremely important. People should know what's happening to formulate decisions. We shouldn't get just one side of the Iraq situation, for example, or for that matter any other country in the world. Our curriculum focus is not on the rote method of learning, but it's on critical thinking. We're challenging students, asking them why do you think this occurred or what would be a better way for that to have happened?

Learners still need to go to school – not necessarily for learning, but for socialisation. I'm a firm believer, especially in the kindergarten to grade 12 schools, that technology is an important adjunct to learning, but the classroom element still needs to be considered. When it comes to adult learners and those actively employed, learners don't have to go to school. The sheer number of courses available online to improve the opportunities and productivity of people in many particular roles is incredible, and there's no reason why one can't go into the work community as an adult and learn online.

In reference to lifelong learning, we recognise that much of the physical and cyber infrastructure available in schools is under-utilised. There's no reason why we can't have classes in schools in the evenings, whether for adult education or basket-weaving, to bring the community into the school and break down barriers. We encourage partnerships, multi-use agreements between communities and schools so that these physical facilities are utilised around the clock. This allows the adult learner to have a centre for education. They especially need encouragement from other adult learners who have taken the plunge in bettering themselves through education, and that encouragement is often valuable.

These partnerships extend beyond the teacher/learner relationship. To help schools change or evolve in terms of reaching families and communities, you should start with the firm commitment that they are a very important part of the school system. To put a child in school from the age of four to eighteen and have them turn out to be a good member of society from a good school system, parents and the community have to take an active involvement. So we encourage parent councils, allowing parents input into the schools; we encourage communities to participate in schools. Schools are not just a physical facility locking its doors at four o'clock and opening them up again at 8.30 the next morning. They have to be a centre for the community.

3.3

### Current curriculum content

In order to become more relevant to the community, the content taught in schools must be current. One of the important things about a curriculum, whether the topic is social studies, maths or English, is timeliness. If you were studying pre-Bush-era Iraq, you wouldn't see what's happening now. You need to ensure that the curriculum is up-to-date and interesting. Students learn in different fashions: the more opportunities they have to learn in different ways, whether through technology, teachers, or auditory types of learning, the better – that's what makes a school system great. The timeliness of curriculum changes is incredibly important: whether they're aged five or seventeen, students like to have relevant information.

I believe strongly in standardised curricula which put across the basic elements of what students learn. It is crucial to provide choices and opportunities in the curriculum to allow these individual learning styles. That does not mean we go back to the seventies open learning system where people learn at their own rates and don't learn if they don't want to. It was shown to be ineffective then because the general rule is that people don't necessarily, of there own volition want to learn or do the work. So there has to be a push from centralised government or a direction of standardisation. What we've done in Alberta is probably a very good mixture: thus 65 per cent of the curriculum is standardised, albeit in numerous forms; and the other 35 per cent is open to the particular school jurisdiction, depending on their particular interest. So for example we have a military academy, a ballet school, an all-girls school, single gender academies – all these different things are in place.

In Alberta, all courses delivered to students are field-tested and screened by us as to content, and each item or element has to be educationally sound. In high school, we have approximately 1,500 courses available to every student. One of the important elements we're moving forwards with technologically – which is going to be a huge adjunct to this – is to move to a centralised, managed, and distributed content server-based system. One of the issues with technology is the overload of information. For example, when a Google search returns 6,372,563 different sites about a particular search topic, no one has the time or willingness to go through all these and find the best material. But a centralised system allows my staff in the Department of Education to screen materials, resources and learning objects before putting them onto the network. Teachers can then look at the server, go into the programmes and easily verify that it's educationally sound. We've decreased the amount of time needed for teachers to research different resources. They know the resource is educationally sound, pedagogically correct, and relevant to what they're teaching so they can then make decisions about what individual students need and desire in their learning efforts. Logically, the next step is personalisation.

## Learning styles and personalisation

Personalisation is the way of the future. We have to grab a learner and let them play and learn with their skills. We've all seen people in the classroom who have high IQs but for various reasons aren't learning in school. Realistically, the school system of the 1950s and 60s, and in some cases the 90s, is aimed at the average student, but we must recognise that there are bright students who need to be challenged. The need to be challenged is a fundamental element of human psychology. We therefore must build a curriculum to challenge these students. But, equally we need to consider those below average. Rather than consigning them to the societal scrapheap, we must find ways to grab them, discover what they're interested in, exploit those interests and bring them forward. The days when teachers stood in front of a class, aimed a lesson at the average student and had everyone come up, down or conform to that level and method of delivery are over.

Our current generation doesn't have different learning styles than previous generations: there have always been different learning styles. Those that didn't conform to the learning style presented to them were either smart or dumb and were classified accordingly. If you had an auditory learner or a visual learner, for example, these expertises were not exploited. They were considered useless, because they didn't conform to the way the lesson was being taught. In actual fact, almost every student has expertise and different learning styles and we have to capture those styles and put them forward. I don't believe that it's different now than when you and I went to school. It's just recognised now and it wasn't previously. When I went to school in the sixties, the teacher divided the room into the 'smart' ones sitting on one side and the 'dumb' ones on the other. There was no recognition that so-called 'dumb' pupils simply learned differently and did not learn in the environment presented to them.

The same phenomenon is occurring in medicine. In previous generations people – family members – just died. Now people die of something, and that's because we have the technology and expertise to recognise why people die. Flipping that analogy over to the learning system, we have the technology and expertise to recognise why people aren't learning and if we can answer the question why people aren't learning, we can also work out what will make them learn. That's where individualised learning is going to become prevalent in our education system.

---

'We have the technology and expertise to recognise why people aren't learning and if we can answer the question why people aren't learning, we can also work out what will make them learn.'

---

If we look at individualised learning, at exploiting the skills of each individual child, then content and assessment have to be geared in that direction. A phenomenon currently occurring in education is that boys aren't doing as well as girls. It's not that boys are not as smart as girls, but that their learning styles are different. So we have to find out how boys learn and set our curriculum in response to that. Boys are more involved in fantasy games, so an exercise in physics about a space alien may more likely cause a boy to learn than a girl to learn. We need to gear curricula towards the individualised learning styles that are out there. The ultimate goal of assessment is to have our children learn and attain knowledge. It doesn't matter how they attain it. Regardless of learning style, their learning assessments should reveal whether or not they've learnt the subject. Counting two space aliens plus three space aliens still equals five, as compared to saying two Barbie dolls plus three Barbie dolls equals five. This implies a higher level of preparation for our teachers.

3.3

It is critical that teachers have degrees and have been taught at a university level. We can then make the information available to the teacher as to what different demographics mean, such as gender bias, boys versus girls, aboriginal versus non-aboriginal. Aboriginal learners have different styles of learning and need to be presented with different elements. The content and approach can then be broken down according to individual students – visual learners, auditory learners etc. We have tests that can determine these traits. Currently, we constantly follow up on achievement tests to find out how these particular students are actually doing. We have the ability to track a student throughout the school system to see if there are different ways they should be taught. While there are many different resources available for teachers, we first need good-quality teachers who recognise the differences in learning styles for each and every student.

A teacher with 25–30 students has to identify the important individual demographics and their respective learning styles. Once that's done, resources are available for the teacher to utilise. Aboriginal children have a different set of requirements when it comes to learning so a teacher has to be specifically prepared in aboriginal teaching. The same applies to boys versus girls.

---

'Technology is the element that is dramatically changing an institution that hasn't significantly changed in the past 80 years.'

---

As a result of these insights an important requirement in Alberta is our contractual agreement with universities regarding necessary knowledge skills and attributes that teachers must have when graduating from the education system. This year we introduced five new knowledge skills and attributes for teachers: technology, aboriginal learners, special needs learners, large-scale assessment (for example, interpreting achievement scores – they have to know how to utilise that data to best effect) and most recently, second languages.

### Preparing teachers for the future

One of the things we pride ourselves on in Alberta is our series of professional development. We have roughly 10–15 full days of professional development for teachers, and they're required to take professional development courses. We know that any education system is only as good or poor as its teachers, and to increase the quality of teachers is one of our most important tasks. Statistically 20 per cent of teachers are early adopters who will utilise technology immediately; another 40-50 per cent will say 'this is wonderful' and learn how to use it eventually; and the other 30 per cent may never see these opportunities. There is little we can do about that. They'll go through the system and have a difficult time in it. However, when we plan for a second education system over for the next 20 years we expect that as the university teachers come in they will have those skills and attributes and will feed into the education system. Veteran teachers are wonderful in what they do and a lot of what they have developed over the years has been instinctive, but now, with all the resources available, we need to move on and equip them with these significant new resources.

In twenty years' time, I envisage teachers as being coordinators, working with individual students on individual problems but not necessarily standing in the front lecturing: a lot of that would be available through technology, so we'd have lectures from experts. For example, why not get a Nobel Prize winner to give Alberta's students a lecture in physics? Teachers would provide appropriate content for various learning student styles; give help on specific problems, and while moving from student to student at their desk, interacting with other resources and technology. The learning system will combine all that. Technology is the element that is dramatically changing an institution that hasn't significantly changed in the past 80 years.

We're putting video conference suites in every school. Why couldn't the best teacher in the province give a lecture on something students are expected to learn over the next week? They would lecture on Monday, and then each individual teacher would act as the coordinator, helping students with the concepts that were presented and helping them learn. By taking this approach we have to assess the general amount of knowledge each student possesses, and then standardise so we can compare the assessments; comparing student A to the provincial standards or to student B to see that they're in fact learning the general concepts. An assessment has to be individualised so it can ascertain that boys and girls or other differentiated learners are mastering the concepts even if in different fashions. The assessment has to test for knowledge of the concept as opposed to a 'what's the capital of Iraq?' fact recitation-based approach.

I see a blurring of boundaries between curricula as it moves into that newer model of the coordinator along with the subject matter experts. We've seen that blurring already. We recognise that fine arts are very important for the developing child's brain, but we don't necessarily have to have a simple fine arts class. We suggest incorporating fine arts into social studies, studying the art of the Inca civilisation while investigating the history of Mexico. It can all be integrated: such as the mathematics of the building of the temples of the Aztecs, the Incas or the Egyptian pyramids.

3.3

We used to present the courses as biology, physics or chemistry for the sciences; but in daily life we don't isolate our subjects, we recognise that chemistry is very intimately related to health, biology, social studies, societal values, and that's the realisation that our education system is coming to and is moving towards. We study history not just to know what happened, but to learn from mistakes and from the positive things that occurred so we can apply those lessons to the future. That kind of integrated learning is going to be the way of the future in education.

### Standards and reporting

Thus, the role of government is essential when it comes to standards; the provision of standardised testing, archiving examination results, and to recognise that there are different levels of difficulty of exams. Individually, one teacher may devise a hard exam; another may make an easy exam in the same course. There has to be standardisation of administration and exam development so we can tell exactly what our children are learning and what their level of competency is. We must ensure that all schools are generating and reporting the same type of information. If we want to compare one particular school with another school from a particular demographic or socio-economic status point of view, we must have the same type of information in a standardised form.

One of the most difficult but simple things we have done in Alberta is giving each student a number, a unique student identifier that stays with them for life. We can now say that student number 137 has finished grade 12 and gone into medicine at the University of Alberta. We can track these students, determine why this student did or did not go to university, or become a successful performer. In turn we should be able to determine at a largely demographic level the directions we need to take to change our system. Further, we can ask what individualised actions could we have taken for student 137 in grade 8 that would have changed their outcomes? Can we apply that information to the next child that comes in with similar issues in grade 8? In northern Alberta we have targeted apprenticeship training to students in grade 8, because that is the age level where it has been shown that they drop out of school or when they lose interest in schooling. Information is not useful information unless it's dependable, standardised and can be repeated. That is the kind of lesson we need to receive from our research into the education system.

These unique identifiers have been applied to all students at all ages. As we only instituted the system two years ago, we do not have complete data, but everything is in place to mine that data for doing exactly that. Forty years from now we will be able to track each individual as to what courses they've taken in our universities and what their interests have been. Obviously privacy is one of the big issues we've had to deal with in this system. That's why we use a non-correlated number rather than a name. We can't specifically identify Joe Bloggs, but what we can say is the person who has these interests has taken these courses and moved into these opportunities. We are doing this to find out statistically the direction in which we need to move. If we have people going into oil and gas technology at age 47, we need to tailor our courses for them. Given this, we need more distance learning because they need to keep a job while they're going to school, so we must make that available to them. This has been a huge step forward for us and has a tremendous amount of potential.

This unique student identifier doesn't retain data associated with learning styles or learning disabilities. You could build that data in, but we haven't yet. It's more of a registration type, but there's no reason why we can't add helpful information later. But again, we're concerned about people's privacy and we're walking a delicate line. Certainly you can read into it a lot of information such as marks, but it's not explicitly stated. From a policy perspective, to have accepted the big issue was privacy. In Alberta we have a Privacy Commissioner and we worked very closely with him to ensure that privacy wouldn't be violated.

### The Alberta Initiative for School Improvement
Four years ago we established a programme called the Alberta Initiative for School Improvement, with funding of $68 million per year. I asked teachers to become our researchers, looking at different ways to improve schools and school achievement. If it's changing the way kids are taught, changing professional development, they are to experiment with it and we will pay for it and support it. I only expect 20% of these programmes to show any benefit; if a programme does not show benefit, it still teaches us something. Perhaps it breaks down a myth about the way children learn. The Alberta Initiative has been an incredible success. We have undertaken over 1,200 projects in the past four

years and many more are coming up, from class size, school lunches, school uniforms and professional development. All these things are interrelated.

In recent surveys, Alberta has topped the list of educational entities worldwide. The critical factor has been our recognition that we do not have a perfect system. We look at research and make changes according to that research: we're flexible enough to embrace change rather than going against it. We have to recognise that we can always improve, while emphasising an environment of constant quality and improvement into the system and continually evaluating what we do, advancing good research and moving ahead with it.

---

'Preparing our students for the workforce, and being good, active participating members of society: that's what this is all about – it is about constant improvement.'

3.3

---

Ultimately, standardised testing is a key issue. Governments need an idea of what their children are learning and how well they're performing. Secondly, I would suggest flexibility in teaching to different learning styles. Teaching systems aimed at the average student are just not going to excel. Schools have to individualise learning styles for the individual student. Thirdly we must provide choice. Students know best what they want to do and a student who goes into a course because they want to is going to be much more successful than a student who goes into a course because they're forced to. Finally, technology is going to revolutionise the future for education. I think the whole idea of having real-time learning, learning about what is happening on the front page of the newspaper, is going to be incredibly powerful when it comes to citizenry, preparing our students for the workforce, and being good, active participating members of society: and that's what this is all about – it is about constant improvement.

### Embracing technology

One of the criticisms I have of anything that purports to rank one country against another is that people tend to rest on their laurels. They say 'we're number one, we're doing wonderfully well', but that doesn't mean they can't do even better. The whole approach of continuous improvement, quality assurance, moving in the direction that research tells us, is going to be the way of the future. When it comes to technology, there are two choices. One can either regard it as just a flash in the pan and ignore it; or it can be embraced with the realisation that when our students graduate they're going to be working with networked technology and computers and therefore must know how to use them, and more importantly, how to get knowledge and information by intelligently using technology. That is the key to technology in education: it's not technology for technology sake; it's technology for knowledge's sake.

# Putting an end to computer-lab thinking

**Ádám Horváth** | IT adviser to the Ministry of Education, Hungary

**Ádám Horváth, IT adviser to the Ministry of Education in Hungary, explains how Hungary's unique position in the EU has led to the development of some unusual IT approaches to education.**

The smartest wrestlers, so they say, use the bulk and momentum of their opponents to bring them down. The harder they come, the harder they fall… It's a strategy we've used with particular effectiveness in Hungary and, as I hope to explain here, perhaps nowhere more so than in the field of education and information technology.

Our country is in a double-bind: we're land-locked and language-locked. We have seven countries on our borders and no outlet to the sea. The Hungarian language belongs to the esoteric Uralic family (we share common linguistic roots with Finnish and, for the curious, with Samoyed, Ugric and Lapp). Uralic tongues are particularly inaccessible to foreigners, especially those of a Latinate disposition.

The Internet should enable us to transcend our geographical restraints but it is, as you may have noticed, predominantly an English-speaking environment. Most Europeans adopt English as their second language, but Hungarians have had challenges here too. Not because English is particularly difficult for us, but because historically it has been more in our interests – for obvious reasons – to learn Russian. And nowadays it tends to be German, since over 30 per cent of our international business is done with that country.

But what goes around, comes around. Hungary was once a dominant power, largely due to its strategic position as the stepping stone between the Balkan Peninsula and the rest of Europe, as well as between the Ukraine and the Mediterranean. Now we're a fully-fledged member of the EU and suddenly our seven neighbours look more like opportunities than challenges. Our GDP is growing strongly at over 3 per cent, our industrial output rose by over 9 per cent in the year to April 2004, and we have a literacy level that most Western nations would envy – and not just in our own language, since our Foreign Language Programme means that in future all students must qualify in at least one other tongue before leaving.

### The access challenge

In this context, what's the education story? In order to join the EU, countries have to submit and receive approval for a National Development Plan. The

Government began work on this at the beginning of 2001; it was adopted in early 2004 and one of the immediate consequences will be the release of funding by the EU to support our initiatives. This funding starts to kick in at the end of 2004, will grow through the next two years, and will wind up in 2013.

My department is responsible for creating an IT strategy for public education and higher education, and for integrating this strategy both upwards (with national IT programmes) and downwards (with individual programmes managed by specific schools and higher-education institutions). We follow through by providing feedback on their implementations, and case-studies for inspiration. We also provide tenders for service supplies and specify the processes involved.

3.4

This strategy was drawn up and approved by the Ministry of Education in the first quarter of 2004. It revolves around the provision of Internet access. This has been a real challenge for Hungary. We have a strong start with a 10Gbs backbone connecting over 85 per cent of our 5,500 schools and colleges. The remainder have to make do with a one-way satellite delivery system, operating at 10-20Mbs and delivering (via a carousel system) material from a cache of the 100 most requested sites.

Our plans revolve around four initiatives: providing Internet connectivity; providing schools with PCs and other ICT equipment; promoting the development of digital content and finally, of course, training our teachers. The PCs are vital: currently we have around one PC being shared by 20–25 students and we would like to increase this as much as possible, initially to 10–12 students per computer.

But there's another challenge that impacts on our work but is not really our responsibility: Internet access in the home. Our main objective must be to prepare students for the marketplace and for lifelong learning, by leveraging the power of the Net and placing greater emphasis on the process of intelligent discovery and research, rather than on the passive processes of being taught. So it is particularly frustrating if – at the end of the day – the student can only apply this skill at school. Unfortunately, Internet access at home remains expensive at around 10,000 forints per month (that's almost $50 at the time of writing). Since Hungary's average wage is about 30 per cent of the EU average and VAT is running at 25 per cent, that's a significant drain on household income.

Meanwhile, back at school, despite the backbone provision, the 'last mile' is reaching only half the students in primary and secondary education at the time of writing. We expect this to be remedied by the end of 2005, thanks to a large project being carried out in conjunction with the Ministry of Informatics and Telecommunication within Hungary. This will bring 1.4 million students in primary and secondary education and 300,000 students in the higher education system online, together with their teachers (about 320,000 in all).

Our solution to the home/school divide has been to change the role of the school in the community. We're transforming our educational centres into community centres, with Internet access for both parents and children. This not only helps to solve the home-access problem, but also creates new opportunities for lifelong learning. The initiative is already proving popular and now we're not only providing basic Internet services, but moving towards the creation of digital learning tools for adults as well as children. For example, we're currently developing driving and language tuition models for parents, with more to come.

That seems to us to be a good example of taking a problem and using it to create new opportunities: providing new roles for our schools, integrating them more effectively into the community, and promoting lifelong learning. The harder they come...

## Speaking in tongues

The same principle can be seen in the teaching of foreign languages. As I've already mentioned, we're introducing requirements for compulsory foreign language skills. At the same time, we have a very underdeveloped industry in Hungary for the development of digital teaching materials. We've turned these two challenges on their heads.

First, the Minister of Education has initiated an EU project that will result in increased local development as part of an EU-wide movement to create a pool of shared teaching materials. In 2003 we started a US$4 million project to develop digital content covering all subjects currently included in the digital curriculum, i.e. history, literature, physics and biology. This material will all be in Hungarian. At the same time, as part of the Hungarian National Development Plan starting in September 2004 (and 66 per cent funded by the EU) we're developing a learning content management system and then from September 2004 we will be buying in more digital content from other countries.

This latter content, however, will *not* be in Hungarian. Instead, we're training teachers to use the foreign materials not only as modules for teaching physics, maths, etc, but also as foreign language tools. In other words, rather than teaching the language on its own, we would like to teach mathematics and physics, for example, in English or in German. It's much easier to learn the language in the context of learning something else.

This approach is already generating enormous interest and enthusiasm. There are some drawbacks: you can't apply the method to all topics (history, for example, tends to be heavily localised, whereas physics is almost a universal curriculum) and we have to train teachers, who will need dual skills (language and the appropriate discipline). A special programme for this has been drawn up and will start in 2005. So once again, we've taken a challenge and used it to create a new opportunity.

### Winning at cards

As a final example, let's take issues of authentication and authorisation. Our educational system is quite conservative and inefficient. This is hardly surprising, given our recent history. Our traditional social structure collapsed during the First World War, then fell under Communist rule, and only began liberalisation in 1968. We didn't hold multiparty elections until 1990. This has bequeathed two main legacies, to do with study programmes and monitoring.

---

'We have lots of opportunities, for example, for those who want to become miners, but not so many for those wanting to go into new media.'

3.4

---

Our higher education facilities have traditionally been funded on the basis of attendance. This has made it very difficult to introduce new courses on demand. We have lots of opportunities, for example, for those who want to become miners, but not so many for those wanting to go into new media. To remedy this, the Government is planning to turn the situation on its head and fund the students, not the institutions. Soon, Hungarian students will be able to pick and choose their courses and pay for them themselves. This is going to have a major impact on higher education in this country, including the novel prospect of students choosing to spend their forints on education abroad.

But it's not much good stimulating demand by students if you can't monitor what they want. Our educational system is very poor at collecting and collating information about what it's actually doing. To solve this problem, we're introducing a new smart card system in 2005. These read-write enabled cards will not only integrate with the initiatives I've mentioned before (for example, acting as authentication and personalisation tools for services offered in school/community online centres) but will also provide a great deal of information about demand and supply in education.

This system looks like being extremely cost-effective. The public will be asked to pay a token amount for their cards (encouraging them to take better care of them, although in fact their individual cost is trivial). They will be then be individually logged in to the national infrastructure every time they use their cards. With our history, we're extremely sensitive about civil liberties, of course, and we have a planned system of distributed, isolated databases that will ensure that no single party can monopolise or manipulate individual information.

It's obvious that an individual read-write card could offer tremendous advantages. We will be able to analyse all the processes in education, their associated costs, as well as authenticating and authorising each individual and perhaps, one day, providing them with easy e-payment solutions for the new demand-driven educational economy.

A typical example could include our National Information Service database, which is provided by the Ministry of Education. The content in the service currently comes from both domestic databases and learning programmes provided by companies such as Elsevier and IFI Thomson. We have almost six million articles available in this system with full text, not including the Hungarian materials. This material is available for all Hungarian higher education students, who will now be able to access them not only at school but from any computer, using their card as authorisation.

Hungary has many challenges ahead, but so far we've managed to set them against each other, converting them to opportunities. We're building on a very strong base, with high literacy and a very high proportion of committed students (averaging currently over nine years in education, ahead of countries like France, Spain and Italy). All we need to do now – in common with most Western nations – is raise our population growth, otherwise we'll run out of people to teach! An innovative solution to *that* problem would doubtless be an interesting one…

# Reflections and possibilities

# Learning communities for teachers and students

**Ulf Lundin** | Executive Director of European Schoolnet, Brussels, Belgium

**Ulf Lundin, a former Swedish State Secretary for Education and Cultural Affairs, describes how European Schoolnet promotes ICT in education with the aim of breaking down barriers to learning.**

### The three strands of European Schoolnet

European Schoolnet, an organisation of 26 Ministries of Education established in 1997 to promote the use of ITT in education and record the European dimension in education, currently works along three strands. The first is school networking and school services, which include the European portals we are running for teachers, headmasters and pupils. Together with special events for schools, we also operate three large networks of teachers.

The second strand is policies and practice. We provide insight into policies and practices regarding new technologies in education and act as a gateway to information of this kind with the Ministries of Education.

The third strand is web services and interoperability: we provide web services, particularly to national portals for schools and especially in the area of educational content. We also try to work with the ministries to ensure a common approach towards standards and interoperability. To this end we launched a Learning Interoperability Framework for Europe (LIFE) action. The launch conference brought together 75 people from a large number of companies and the standards organisations.

Regarding the main challenges facing ministries when they adopt ICT policies, we're currently trying to deal with three phases concerning new technologies and education at the same time. The first phase, which has been the focus since the mid-nineties, has been to ensure that computers are correctly implemented in line with our teacher training programme. A lot of progress has been made but we're still far from achieving our ultimate goals and many countries are still only at an exploratory stage.

The second phase, which is becoming well developed in a number of countries, is when technologies are being put to good use within the framework of the existing curriculum and we're focusing on how we can better use resources to link computers to curricula. The whole issue of assessment is strongly connected to this – has investment given the results we expected? – and this is constantly being measured.

Then we have the third phase, which in a sense is the most challenging and which is currently emerging. This is to look into models where we can truly benefit from the technology, which might call for a re-evaluation of the organisational context and of the way schooling and learning are developed or delivered; and also the emergence of different actors in the field from the traditional ones, the state and local government. Of course, each phase represents a challenge in its own right. The ministries need to address these challenges and, with the enlarged Europe, new countries coming into Europe are also in the middle of grappling with them. There are very few ministries that recognise what the real focus should be in the third phase and nobody's really addressing this. I think what is being seen is more an effort at a national level or in very isolated pilots.

4.1

Some countries are more developed in all three phases than others, either because they started early or had more tradition of early technology pickup, although there are elements in different countries. I'm particularly interested in Catalonia, which has established a number of forward-looking measures, but of course it's in very early development. There are some progressive elements in the UK but it's difficult to get a clear sense of where things are going: the impression from the outside is that the reluctance of teachers is more pronounced in the UK than anywhere else. There are new developments in the Nordic countries and Denmark, and the Netherlands is a country where a lot of things could and do happen. It's the least transparent country at the moment in that there are a number of things in place but it's hard to understand what government policy really is and whether, at a national level, you can really talk about an effort to move into new models. The most interesting country is Hungary, which has put definite measures in place, particularly regarding digitising the curriculum.

### Changing the infrastructure

Sweden is easier than most other countries because it has an open, national framework curriculum. There are many opportunities at the local level, the local municipality and the local school to run their own kind of curriculum. This is important because, if you don't have this framework factor in place, you need to look at the structure of the curriculum: if you're running a very centralised curriculum, with a lot of central directives in terms of how you spend the week or what the teachers do exactly during the week, then you'll have far more difficulties in making changes.

If I was still in the Swedish Ministry of Education I would change the infrastructure of the learner and teacher, which has been looked upon as being apart from the institutional and the curricular structure. We need to create a more flexible structure which, from the learner point of view, is quite important. The issue is about where young people are supposed to learn and the answer is of course everywhere. So we need to ensure that we have an institutional, curricular and evaluation framework that can take into consideration learning that has taken place in different environments. A proposal was released recently that firmly reiterates issues around infrastructure and teachers, and what I would have argued if I had been in a policy situation is that we are not using the technology to its potential.

---

**'One of the reasons that schools don't change is that we're still very much into age-related and grade-related classrooms.'**

---

Let me illustrate this: when I was in a decision-making position 25 years ago, one of my tasks was to coordinate the formal national curriculum and I felt that we should give some prominence to technology. So I decided to throw out the subject of typewriting and replace it with a subject called 'datology' – the Swedish word for computer is 'dator'; translated it would be 'computology'. What I didn't realise was that teachers who were brought in to teach that subject were still typewriting teachers. So, in this subject they were actually teaching typewriting but using computers instead of typewriters and I think this was a typical example of the kind of mistake we made and are still making: that we're not building on the true capacity of the technology and of its networking capability and we need to take this much more into consideration.

### The networked school

If I had had the opportunity to start again, the networked school would have been a central focus, with significant consequences for work methods: a networked school is not just a school with a physical network; it means that for each lesson where it's beneficial to do so, you're networked to the appropriate place where the information and ideas of supporting teachers are located. To take science teaching, what's stopping you from having a lesson where you have an active network to a likeminded class in Australia or where research can be linked to a science centre in, say, Denmark to illustrate some physical law or biological experiment?

This to me is the true value of networking. Obviously with technology it calls for many changes, in particular in terms of infrastructure and teachers' attitudes, and also for truly collaborative teams of teachers. You can't really work on your own if you want to take this kind of approach and this might touch on what is a slight problem in current teacher training – that you put in a lot of effort in terms of technology but very little in terms of the new pedagogues who need to benefit from it.

The old type of pedagogy, with teachers who close the classroom door and want to be on their own with their students, is still the situation in many countries. Certainly there are individual approaches and sometimes we're very unfair to teachers because we look at them as a very homogenous group while in reality they're a very heterogeneous group with all sorts of ideas and approaches of their own. But I think the collaborative dimension is quite important. Then, of course, when you start to go into different subjects and look at classroom models, how biology is taught and using new technology, then there are a lot of other things that need to be rethought. At a very basic level we need to agree generally on a kind of pedagogical working model that will allow you to benefit from working technology and this is what the focus on teacher training should be at this stage. We have spent a large amount of money getting teachers to learn how to use a different product from a limited group of companies. In the near future these teachers will have access to virtual learning environments to give them tools that are quite different. They will be working with a method that will automatically make them look at tools from the collaborative angle.

4.1

This collaboration will allow new practices to filter through to local schools and curricula and it's important to find ways to encourage governments to invest in that way of working. And there's another dimension involved, which is that in this open model you may also in some cases be dealing with very mixed groups from an age point of view. We may be talking about something that is very far ahead and maybe in the extra curricular area, but you may well have groups which include upper secondary kids with people already out in working life. So you may have to prepare teachers to work within more heterogeneous groups than they're doing at the moment. One of the reasons that schools don't change is that we're still very much into age-related and grade-related classrooms. I think the area where these changes might appear first, or a better place to find a solution, might be science because that is where the homogenous age group is less obvious. You have young geniuses and old slow-starters.

## Assessment

In the area of assessment we are doing little or nothing. I think this needs to be addressed at a national level and it's not an issue in Europe to the extent where we can really bring together many of the experiences from different countries. I think assessment will be an issue later on and, from a long-term development point of view, this might actually be an advantage because the risk with a very real assessment focus approach in the American model is that you actually lock yourself into the curriculum structure. You're trying to optimise within a framework that might not be the best one. There are two important aspects in terms of content. One is, of course, that the content available in today's textbooks needs to be available in digital format alongside other kinds of material that can be used.

The approach taken in some countries undertaking large-scale digitising efforts or making learning resources available electronically, such as France and Sweden, is important. The Hungarian programme of digitising content is absolutely marvellous and has been responsible for tremendous changes.

### Learning objects

European Schoolnet, in particular, talks about reusable learning objects where teachers work on digital learning material but in a way that makes it possible for the teacher to bring it into the larger context of what they would like to do. We are just at the beginning of the whole development around learning objects but a lot of countries will start to pick up on this in the next 5–8 years. Digitising content isn't just taking the textbook and putting it online. It's trying to do innovative things with it to make learners engage with it more. It's about breaking up textbooks and making them clearly available in small elements, allowing teachers to construct lessons and programmes on their own on the basis of those books. I don't think anyone is working on the notion any longer that you simply take the textbook and put in a little bit of video and that's the new learning content.

In this area Schoolnet have been developing learning objects within the framework of a project called Celebrate, in which we bring together ministries, content providers, and research organisations such as universities to look at the notion of learning objects and make them available to schools as a basis for all pilot work, particularly by publishers participating but also by ministries and teachers themselves. They look at the pedagogical model that could facilitate the use of learning objects in which pedagogical context works to the learning object's advantage but this content also raises the issue of what should be the pedagogical content of learning objectives. The learning object is just a neutral resource, available for or a link to a pedagogical approach which, when you choose the learning object, is automatically implemented and there are other projects looking much deeper into this issue. Then there's the delivery of the learning object. How can you make them available across Europe and across different learning management systems? So, a very substantial effort in the project has been to look into the interoperability issues and system architecture. We have implemented a prototype which was demonstrated to the partners last week.

'The true potential of technology in education is about collaborative working and learning for both teachers and students.'

One of the issues about pedagogical approaches to learning objects is that pedagogues vary across Europe quite considerably and some of the content is not necessarily culturally accessible to all countries. This has been discussed among pedagogical experts in the group but the learning object produced within the framework of the project was selected to be easy to use across Europe; for that reason science is quite strongly featured. The main issue is a linguistic one, for instance how can a learning object produced in Hungary be beneficial for a school in the UK? But some good documents have also been produced. Bob McCormick wrote a paper based on Celebrate called 'Where Is the Pedagogue?' which is very interesting.

A question we must now decide on in the team is the issue of how intelligent learning objects will be addressed, which raises a number of issues: the approach is very much the self-paced learning model and there's almost an industry-driven effort to make the self-paced learning paradigm the predominant one. In self-paced learning you don't need a teacher or need very little help from the teacher. Instead you progress through a course or programme. I think the self-paced learning model is extremely useful in limited situations. It's in an environment where the attitudes and habits that you induce in the learner are much more important; however, self-paced learning has, in my view, severe limitations.

4.1

### Collaborative learning

The true potential of technology in education is about collaborative working and learning for both teachers and students. Sometimes we're looking for something that might not even be there. We're talking about pedagogy in all sorts of mysterious terms when in reality it seems to me to be a quite simple approach of making the collaborative dimension much more prominent by getting teachers to accept and recognise it.

# Challenging change through connectivity

**Alexander Yu Uvarov** | Leading Researcher at The Council on Cybernetics, Russian Academy of Science, Russia

**Alexander Yu Uvarov reflects critically on the influence of connectivity on education.**

Russian school reform has been underway for several decades. Since 1985, documents that are part of the reform agenda have covered computers, new information technologies and the introduction of such technologies into education. Nevertheless, even today the last of those is still often discussed as an optional, purely technical issue, with nothing to do with the essence of reform. Politicians in charge of education often regard computers and the Internet as separate from general problems of the content and methods of education and the way in which the educational process is organised and managed.

Those thinking traditionally fail to see the obvious: that one of the reasons why change is needed both in society and in education is the global effect of IT on the economy.[1] It is hard to realise that applying an information-based approach to education involves more than just putting Internet-connected computers into schools. It is primarily the difficult process of modifying the content, methods and organisational forms of general education at the stage of transfer to the information society. Behind the wall of difficulties experienced by schools today, it is hard to recognise the change that is taking place here and now: the actual transfer from the education we had when access to information was limited, to the education being put in place now, when access to information is free. In today's Russia, it is even more difficult to understand this and to build an adequate strategy of applying IT to the world of education, because the Russian educational system is currently undergoing two quite different crises.

## A recurring theme

An analysis 30 years ago of education development worldwide performed by a research group under the aegis of UNESCO[2] showed that the goal of 'education for all children of school age' would be practically unattainable for many decades to come. The population was growing faster than the number of schools, and the number of children who would have to manage without schooling was increasing. This factor and others were what led Coombs to the conclusion that the world educational system was undergoing a crisis. At that time, teachers in our country were proud of the fact that here, even though difficulties were obvious, everybody received primary education, and secondary education was close to being generally

1. For details, see Uvarov, A.Yu. (1994) New Information Technologies and Reform of Education, Informatics and Education, No. 3.

2. Coombs, P. (1968) The World Educational Crisis: A System Analysis, New York, Oxford University Press.

available, too. By the beginning of the 1980s in the USSR, this serious social problem had officially been solved.[3] General education stopped attracting public attention, and remained a subject of interest only for administrators in charge of organising education.

At the beginning of the new millennium, the problem has become topical again. The lack of funding and of qualified teachers in schools, an increase in the number of homeless children, and the gap between urban and rural areas have all resulted in a recurrence of Coombs' Crisis (CC) in Russia. Among administrative measures aimed at a practical escape from CC, attempts to reform the content of education (in fact, to reduce the requirements stipulated for the results of secondary education) clearly dominate. As far as the use of IT in education is concerned, computers and the Internet are sometimes mentioned as tools providing 'equal access to knowledge' for young people. However, there are no practical (or even serious theoretical) teaching schemes for using new information technologies as a tool to eliminate CC.

At the end of the 1970s, Alvin Toffler, introducing the idea of 'future shock',[4] observed that in agricultural society the way of life remains almost unchanged for generations; in an industrial society, it changes during the lifetime of a generation; and in a post-industrial society, it changes several times during a lifetime. Knowledge and everyday skills taught at school quickly become obsolete. In a traditional school, teachers can no longer be sure that the content of the education they provide to children is what they will need tomorrow. Education requires fundamental updating, and emphasis should be placed on methods of activities instead of a fixed range of knowledge and skills.

### Toffler's crisis

However, our schools and their educational programmes are still oriented towards education's traditional content. This obvious gap can be labelled as Toffler's Crisis (TC). To educational researchers both domestically and abroad, this gap was not unexpected. Developers of the psychological educational theory in our country (including VV Davydov, author of the 'developing education' concept) and in others came to similar conclusions in the 1970s. In the US, for example, one such educational specialist was Seymour Papert, an apologist for constructivist education and a strong advocate of introducing information technologies to schools. It is almost impossible to overcome TC with information technologies used by traditional schools. This task requires

3. At about the same time as Coombs, a Russian sociologist, T.A. Zaslavskaya, demonstrated that in our country this problem is solved by means of 'extended reproduction of mediocrity', which actually devalues secondary education.
4.2

4. Toffler, A. (1978) The Third Wave. New York, Harper and Row.

more than just a better selection of knowledge and skills taught in school; it requires giving up the knowledge-based educational paradigm completely. And even though most authors of educational reform admit this in theory, it is hard to implement, as the model for schools that will be able to meet the challenges of modified education content is still being developed.

During the Industrial Revolution, printing and textbooks led to revolutionary changes in 'pre-industrial education', allowing the establishment and development of modern mass schooling, meeting requirements imposed on a well-organised enterprise with a strictly fixed closed educational architecture, which has more or less successfully fulfilled its mission for many decades. Despite its obvious drawbacks, this architecture is still viable. Its establishment is a result of the work of many generations of great teachers. It was a huge social achievement, which met the requirements of its epoch, making schools all over the civilised world essentially similar.

## Closed educational architecture

The advantages and disadvantages of the closed educational architecture could be seen particularly clearly in the work of the Soviet unified general school, where its principles were implemented most consistently.[5] This is the key reason both for the generally recognised achievements of the Soviet school and for the problems with its reform today. The fixed technology of the educational process (neither teachers, school, local educational authorities, students nor public were allowed to modify technological standards set by the single technological centre), a limited set of available teaching aids (which teachers were obliged to know and use), restrictions imposed on the variation of information available (all students had the same textbooks) and strict normative regulation of all participants' activities (which, in particular, prevented the distribution of drugs in school) not only satisfied ideological requirements, but also were well supported by traditional information technologies. Thus, activities within the educational system were fixed, and centralised manipulation of facts allowed strict control of the entire content of the educational process.

A closed educational architecture establishes a minimum level of general education, thus creating a barrier against low-quality teaching and ensuring regular mass professional development for teachers. It allows the relatively effective introduction of global modifications to the educational process. An illustration of this effectiveness is the introduction of a new subject, Informatics, which took two years (1985–86). It was introduced simultaneously at all schools in the country, despite the passive opposition of most teachers. We were all students of this schooling, and so far it has not changed much.

While speaking of the positive aspects of the closed educational architecture, we must also realise its drawbacks. They are to a substantial degree a continuation of its advantages; they are widely known, and their description and analysis can easily be found in modern literature on educational science.[6] The closed architecture was created to provide mass education in a situation where

5. In the 1920s, Soviet teachers tried to create a 'school of the future' that would switch to an open architecture of education; but their attempts failed, partly because their ideas were ahead of their time.

6. See, for example, Dneprov, E.D. (1994) Fourth School Reform. Moscow Interpraks.

access to information is limited. Today, the situation is quickly changing, and the closed architecture of the traditional school is beginning to conflict with students' unlimited access to information. It is slowly becoming obsolete, together with the industrial society in which it was born. This is happening in all developed and developing countries throughout the world, not only in Russia. For example, Davydov's theory of developing education, which requires a revision of many dogmas from traditional schooling, is equally popular in Russia and abroad.

In the developing information society, access to information cannot be restricted. Free access to the entire wealth of information accumulated by mankind is everyone's undeniable right. This right is not only declared, but is also secured by up-to-date electronic mass media and the global infrastructure of the Internet. The key task that schooling faces today is to teach people to live and work in this quickly changing environment. This means that existing methods and forms of teaching should change the extent to which they include components of the new content of education.[7]

4.2

7. For example, the traditional frontal form of work whose idea is to teach students to obey should also be supplemented by teamwork so that students learn group-work techniques and get used to co-operation.

---

'Free access to the entire wealth of information accumulated by mankind is everyone's undeniable right.'

---

The updated content of education, combined with computers supporting it, is the basis of all new-generation educational programmes that we should offer to today's students, future members of the information society. However, people often fail to realise that this process is mainly slowed down by modern didactics, existing school organisation, and the closed architecture of education. Traditional schooling, created when the industrial society was being formed, was the key source of positive information about the world we live in; but now it is slowly vanishing. The image of school as the main, indisputable source of positive knowledge for young people has been destroyed. Everybody is dissatisfied with the traditional organisation of school. This constantly growing dissatisfaction, on the one hand, and the growing influence of communication and information services vendors upon society on the other hand, inevitably create conditions under which the exclusive role of the modern general school as the key agent of socialisation is disputed. Commercial e-learning projects are already being discussed as an alternative to the traditional general school. And even though the practical implementation of such projects is still remote, it is about time teachers became aware of the dilemma that the modern school as an institutional setting is facing for the first time:

• either it can fundamentally change and drastically increase its importance and prestige, becoming once again the leading force for social development and the rearrangement of society; or

• it can slowly and painfully leave the scene, replaced by parents' communities and new educational institutions based on services offered by enterprising content providers over the Internet.

In order to regard the current situation in education as transitional, nothing less than a new paradigm of thinking is required. This is the main reason why politicians in charge of education find it hard to make adequate decisions. Within the framework of traditional thinking, the world of school is very simple: scientists develop educational programmes, then prepare manuals and teaching guidelines (which are today's alternatives). They are submitted to the Teaching Techniques Department of the Ministry for expert assessment, they are recommended for use in schools, and teachers follow these recommendations in their teaching. Ten years ago, teachers had one to three manuals to choose from.

Today, in a democracy, the choice is wider. This is one result of the authorities' granting permission to teachers to be creative. Teachers have even been allowed to develop their own experimental curricula, which are then subject to discussion and approval. Teachers in general obviously have neither time, energy nor the skills required to write their own manuals. However, once in a while teachers do write such a manual, and they then follow a well-known route: they have it discussed at the Teaching Techniques Department and approved, and then use (or even publish) it. Officially, restrictions imposed on the nature of the educational environment at the local level have been mitigated, but essentially nothing has changed. On the other hand, teachers sometimes do not receive their salary on time, so they are not too eager to take on creative work.

### Localising content

Between the ministry and teachers is the administrative system. Regional educational authorities have taken up their right to participate in building a regional component to the education content, along with its related expert assessment and publication of manuals. Declaring that they are 'democratising schools' and 'taking into account local conditions', local authorities fight with federal authorities for their right to command their portion of the 'educational pie'. Once in a while, it is local authorities and teaching-techniques departments that control school work. In order to protect themselves from the formal system, schools adhere to established standards.

Much can be said about the way in which the general political process of building democracy in Russia is naturally reflected in the educational system. Everyone who works at a school knows this story well. It mirrors values, beliefs and techniques characteristic of today's educational system. That is why information-based programmes like the one approved by the Ministry of Education last summer are no surprise. Developers of the programme, just like many officials, were thinking within the framework of traditional closed educational architecture.[8]

8. For more information, see Uvarov, A.Yu. (2001) Rural School and the Internet. Educational Informatics No. 2.

In the closed architecture, active architects are allowed to introduce changes they consider necessary in the organisation of the educational process. However, these architects are themselves outside school. The system passes their decisions along to the people who are to carry them out, and teachers are required to follow these decisions by all possible means. With this approach, the system was totally right when, for example, it punished teachers who 'deviated from the scheme'. Sukhomlinsky[9] and innovative teachers first had to occupy positions as official system architects (for example, by joining the Teaching Academy), and only then could they get down to creative work. Within the paradigm of a closed architecture of education, this is justified. Within the open architecture, the right to determine the real progress of the learning process belongs to the school.

9. V.A. Sukhomlinsky, Russian pedagogue 1918–1970.

## Open architecture

The architecture of education can be open for students or for teachers (depending on who determines the learning process). In the first case, emphasis is placed on self-education: in the second, on a more active role for the teacher. In order to implement an open architecture for students, a corresponding learning scheme needs to be established for them. In this case, they will be able to take over a substantial part of the responsibility for educational results. This approach is natural for university and senior-school students.

4.2

'Much can be said about the way in which the general political process of building democracy in Russia is naturally reflected in the educational system.'

For junior students, the second approach is more natural. In this case, the architects of the educational process are teachers, who should be given as much freedom as possible. For instance, they may conduct a lesson using 'hot' material from the news programme they watched in the morning. Those who have to deal with school students every day were the first to feel that life had changed: both the world and children are now different. It is very hard to work in the old ways.[10] Professional teachers have to improvise, search and use new approaches in their work.[11] And they are absolutely right to do so, for there is nobody else to help them. On the other hand, teachers' salaries are low, there are too many students per class, classrooms urgently require decoration and re-equipment, funds spent for administrative support are very limited, and it is very hard to expect teachers to deal with the variety of unsolved teaching problems unaided. It is hard to expect that a wide range of effective techniques and teaching aids, the building units of educational architecture, will appear out of the blue (as a result of the magic action of the 'educational market'); or to expect difficult problems in the practical reform of education to get solved by themselves. Teachers cannot do this job unless Internet specialists, teaching-aids development experts, authorities, students and students' parents help them, and unless special training is provided.

10. To use an analogy: today's situation in school is a classic revolutionary one, as 'lower classes' cannot live the old way, while 'upper classes' cannot lead or support the necessary changes. This is no surprise, as the transfer to the information society really is a revolutionary one.

11. Of course, they did not do it alone. They were supported by a group of specialists in educational innovation.

In order to solve this problem, all relevant knowledge developed anywhere in the world so far should be used.

The open architecture of education provides an additional resource, helping to solve constantly emerging daily problems. Under new conditions, traditional manuals prove fairly useless. The reason is not the lack of teaching aids or techniques; on the contrary, the volume of materials used has grown enormously and computers are therefore required. The Internet is needed, too, as it provides training information (students should solve problems and conduct research), serves as an environment where results obtained can be published, enables teachers working at different schools to exchange current information, allows a teacher to invite a specialist to attend a lesson, and offers ways to do many other useful things.

Methodical course development in this new generation is characterised by a substantial volume of constantly growing, excess material; a modular structure; much activity performed independently by students during lessons; the possibility of quickly modifying the curriculum to reflect current conditions (and teachers' qualifications); students working together as a team; and intensive use of information technologies. Regular communication with other teachers and teaching techniques specialists promotes the formation of a professional teachers' community, who solve their professional issues in an open and responsible way. Each teacher's methodical inventions and developments are available to all, and methods can quickly be checked and approved by colleagues. An online professional community is formed, which can become an effective intermediary between teachers and educational bodies and help schools transfer to effective operation in the information society.

---

'The transforming Internet in the transforming society will also require schools to transform.'

---

In the information epoch, school teachers need a wide selection of well-organised, easily available materials. To reduce the amount of speaking and to be able to teach students to learn, teachers need special self-teach materials (including multimedia and video resources). The paradigm of the closed architecture of education is based on the assumption that the teaching-techniques specialist from the ministry knows better than anyone else what should be done in the classroom. The paradigm of the open architecture envisages the transfer of both resources and the responsibility to the teacher, who performs the entire job. To be able to bear this responsibility and become architects of the learning process, teachers need numerous 'construction units': training texts, educational software, electronic encyclopaedias, all of it easily available here and now. Assessment tools are changing, too. Students can perform tasks not only 'for the teacher' but also for many significant others by publishing results on the Internet. Assesment by publicity is the most exacting assessment of all.

Transfer to the open architecture of education with a wide use of Internet technologies provides a natural solution for many problems long suffered by schools. This is the only effective means of making schools information-based. However, there is no 'royal route': much methodical work is required, as well as the retraining of teachers and the reorganisation of the entire educational infrastructure. But in this way, information technologies are built in as an essential tool, and schools teach students to live real lives in the information society.

## The post modern school

A school in the post-industrial society is a post-modern school. It is not a 'unified general labour/polytechnic school', but consists of many different schools having very little in common. Out of this controllable variety, a new general post-industrial school will be born – a school with an open education architecture, one where education will not only be declared, but will actually be individual. The Internet is a post-modern phenomenon, too. Unlike school, it has no history. But the problems of the society that is now coming into being are global and individual at the same time, and any unprejudiced user and explorer can see them readily via the Internet. Many problems that are being heatedly discussed in relation to the Internet (freedom, responsibility, self-discipline and other 'self' issues) are traditional ones for education. Some Internet pioneers understand that school and the Internet have a great deal in common, despite all their differences as institutional settings, and that they will substantially influence each other.

4.2

Speaking of the influence of educational problems on the development of the Internet, John Chambers, CEO of Cisco Systems, recently said that e-learning, as it develops, will fundamentally change the Internet we know today.[12] The transforming Internet in the transforming society will also require schools to transform. The slow, difficult but inevitable transfer to a school system with an open architecture of education is a bilateral process, which ensures both the development of schools under the influence of the Internet and a contribution of schools to the development of the Internet.

12. Galagan, P.A. (2001)
The Cisco e-learning story,
Training and Development,
#552, pp. 46–55.

# Networking for transformation: a vision for the future

**David Triggs** | Principal, Greensward College, England

**David Triggs argues that the need to 'transform' schools into Networked Virtual Learning Organisations has never been greater. Major demographic changes, shifting working life patterns and global employment are just three key drivers that will force governments to transform not only their education provision but the whole of their public services delivery.**

I n the UK, live births are at a level well below that required to provide a sustainable workforce past 2020. Demographic trends show that during the next twenty years the number of people over the age of 65 will exceed the number of people aged under 16. Accordingly, the UK Government should give careful consideration to the type and location of schools it is about to build or refurbish under the provision of the 'Building Schools of the Future'[1] programme. The investment of over £15 billion during the next 15 years is a one-off opportunity to provide education that will not only ensure that young people in the UK achieve world-class learning outcomes but that they will be able to become part of the workforce while still in full-time compulsory education.

1. Details of 'Building Schools for the Future' can be found at http://www.dfes.gov.uk/pns/DisplayPN.cgi?pn_id=2004_0025

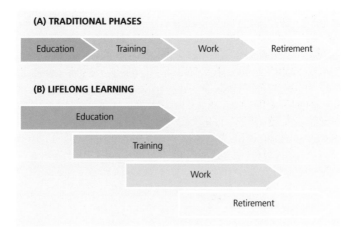

**(A) TRADITIONAL PHASES**

Education → Training → Work → Retirement

**(B) LIFELONG LEARNING**

Education

Training

Work

Retirement

Figure 1 shows the shifting pattern of our working/learning lives.

Example A shows the linear process that has been the traditional route through life for many years. Example B, however, shows the changing nature of education, training, work and retirement. In the late 1960s I was told by the careers teacher that I would change jobs or careers perhaps three times during my working life. The Connexions Service[2] is now advising young

2. The Connexions service provides confidential advice and support to 13–19 year olds. See http://www.connexions-direct.com/

people that they can now expect to change jobs or careers ten or more times. It is clear, therefore, that if the UK and other Western countries are to remain competitive and indeed solvent there will need to be a radical rethink of the form and process of secondary education.

### The Digital Harbour

In the late 1990s Professor Brian Caldwell of the Education Faculty of Melbourne University, Australia was involved in a project to build the world's first 'Digital Harbour'. The aim of this project was to build a state-of-the-art school in the centre of Melbourne's Docklands regeneration programme. The vision was for students both registered at the school as well as those from outlying schools to spend time at the Digital Harbour but more importantly engage in work-related learning in the many technology and communication companies that were building offices and data centres within the Dockland area.

4.3

We can now see just how visionary Professor Caldwell and his colleagues were. As the demographic time-bomb descends upon the UK it will be crucial that government recognises the challenge and begins the process of engaging with private industry to relocate schools, colleges and universities on to business parks, within city office blocks or in industrial centres. Young people must be encouraged to develop as social and business entrepreneurs, and the development of industry standards such as Cisco's CCNA award will become the norm not the exception. Blended learning co-ordinated by 'knowledge managers' will replace traditional classes where the now redundant teacher seeks to protect but reluctantly share knowledge.

Government will need to reconsider what they mean by 'world-class learning outcomes'. Will they be just the traditional academic courses or will we at least begin to realise that if we are to compete on a global stage we need a far more extensive, industry-standard range of qualifications?

### Turbo-learning

Young people growing up in the Western world can increasingly be described as 'MTV kids'. From an early age, they have become acclimatised to a video, digital, web-based world. Their key methods of communication with their friends are via MSN Messenger, SMS text messaging or email. Young people today can multitask in ways that their parents and grandparents cannot imagine. It is not unusual to see a teenager answering text messages, communicating via MSN, listening to music while watching the TV all at the same time. Schools, however, have by and large not kept pace with the digital world. Too often we see teachers standing at the chalk or white board asking their students to 'copy off the board'. The use of digital media is still the exception not the rule and today's young people cannot understand why they have to be taught with the same pedagogy as their parents and grandparents. Accordingly we see increased numbers of student who have become the 3Ds; the disaffected, disengaged and disappeared.

Today's young people are discerning learners; if they are to be engaged and successful in the learning process we need to ensure their voices are listened to. This engagement process will see a move to 'turbo-learning' as opposed to the more traditional 'teaching and learning' or 'chalk and talk' we have witnessed for generation. Turbo-learning will include the use of multimedia, sound, video, experiential learning via computer simulations, Flash animation and other communication tools. Personalised learning and the development of the individual's learning skills will have to push aside outdated teaching styles and methods. Greater awareness of students' learning styles must replace rote learning and personalised learning for every student must become the aim of every learning institution.

It will not be enough for young people to leave school with their five or more A-C grades at GCSE at the age of sixteen or three Advanced levels at eighteen. We must ensure that all our learners of the future know how to learn and be assured that as they train for their next job they can order their learning and have it delivered at the right price, right quality and at the right time. Schools must, therefore, become learning centres for local, national and international communities. We must strive to create schools where students are using a range of applications and curriculum materials, online information and knowledge as a routine component of the education process. They must become learning organisations that demonstrate the use of leading edge models and are able to show leadership and innovation in the area of learning technologies. And they must become dynamic learning communities, where students are stimulated and knowledge managers are facilitators of learning and knowledge management.

### Knowledge management strategies

As we develop knowledge managers (teachers), they must be capable of employing a wide and innovative range of knowledge management strategies, creating learning environments that address the needs and aspirations of all students. They must have the ability to use innovative practice to deliver the twenty-first-century curriculum, assisting students to seek and manage knowledge. Successful knowledge managers will be able to monitor and plan the learning process and programmes of individual students with access to an extensive collection of learning support materials and a worldwide network of professional colleagues and mentors via the Internet. They will seek to work with colleagues in other locations around the world, sharing professional and curriculum development activities and expertise. They will also take on new professional roles as mentors, facilitators, project coordinators and curriculum developers made possible through the Internet.

If the UK is to meet the challenges of the early twenty-first century we will need students who are engaged in the learning process, participating in a more varied range of learning activities matched to their individual needs, interests and capabilities.

---

'Learners of the future will be capable of acquiring knowledge, skills and attitudes which will be essential for a successful and fulfilling life in this millennium.'

---

Learning will be in an international environment characterised by collaborative work, problem-solving and effectively communicating ideas, taking greater responsibility for their own learning and assuming new roles in supporting and mentoring peers and assisting their knowledge managers. Young people will need to broaden their horizons and become global citizens, accessing resources and working with peers and mentors across the world via the Internet. Learners of the future will be capable of acquiring knowledge, skills and attitudes which will be essential for a successful and fulfilling life in this millennium as well as becoming regular, competent and discriminating users of technology in their daily activity of learning and managing knowledge.

4.3

### Networked Virtual Learning Organisations

To facilitate this we must seek to build Networked Virtual Learning Organisations (NVLOs) that have an infrastructure that can provide the learning experience for our twenty-first-century learners. Every school must have a 1Gbs Local Area Network to carry multimedia learning materials, which will extend into every classroom. Where possible a wireless network will overlay the hard wiring to facilitate 'anytime, anywhere learning' on the NVLO site. All teachers must be issued with a high-quality notebook or tablet PC, and classrooms across the country must be fitted with a digital projector. It is futile to believe that teachers will develop the skills required to become knowledge managers if we do not provide them with the appropriate tools and resources, which will allow them to take responsibility for their own learning and development.

Government and educationalists must engage in futures thinking if we are to develop a society for the future and a workforce which will keep the UK at the forefront of technological development. Perhaps one of the best examples of futures thinking was demonstrated by Bill Gates, CEO of Microsoft. In his book *Business at the Speed of Thought* (1999), he describes the 'incisors' he used to help a group of business-people understand why they needed to engage in futures thinking. In less than five years his vision has come to fruition and the future has arrived even if it is not evenly distributed. Today we see the following has come true: he asked them to agree or disagree with the following statements:

- people at work use computers every day for the majority of their jobs;
- paperwork is increasingly being replaced by more efficient digital administrative processes;
- most households will have computers;
- computers are becoming as common in homes as telephones or TVs;
- most businesses and most households have high speed connections to the World Wide Web;
- e-mail is increasingly becoming as common a method of communication among people in business and homes as the telephone or paper mail were in the past;
- consumer bills now often arrive electronically;
- many people now make their travel arrangements over the Internet;
- digital appliances have become commonplace;
- digital devices for photography, video, TV, phones are becoming ubiquitous;
- other digital devices now proliferate around the home and are connected to the Web.

If we agree with all these statements we must challenge our education system to provide the skills and experiences for our learners that will meet Bill Gates's challenge. With the support of Cisco Systems we have developed the Networked Virtual Learning Organisation model (see Figure 2).

At the heart of this model is World Class Learning Outcomes. Individual schools, district education authorities can determine their own World Class Learning Outcomes and this model then seeks to offer a platform for delivery of those outcomes. The next circle sets out the key aspects, which any schools must strive to achieve the highest standards, eg teaching, learning and links with parents and the community. Circle three is the technological framework required through which to develop twenty-first-century edutainment. Next we have examples of partnerships that must be formed will not only deliver high-quality learning experiences but also bring together other public services including health, children's service and education. Finally we see examples of the types of results that can be achieved if we work coherently. These results include the traditional educational results but more importantly they will provide an increasing range of industry standard results.

The NVLO model is offered as a simple route map for the development of a platform from which educational transformation can take place. It is not intended to be definitive and does not seek to determine the pedagogy or curriculum. Through an emphasis on the employment of learning technologies,

**NETWORKED VIRTUAL LEARNING COMMUNITY**

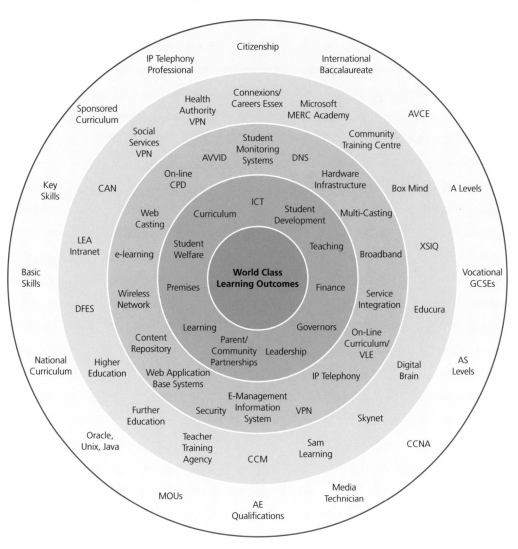

Figure 2
Networked Virtual Learning
Organisation model

the NVLO model seeks to create a partnership between the public, private and commercial sectors aimed at facilitating the education changes that the twenty-first century demands. As with all technologies, learning technologies must be viewed as accelerators and enablers of learning, not a panacea to learning in their own right.

The sociologist B.W. Huebsch stated that, 'this is an age of change. Never before in the history of mankind have so many and so frequent changes occurred.' He made that statement in 1922, but the sentiment remains as true today as it was then. The current education format has been employed for over 130 years but the twenty-first century will not be as generous or forgiving to those countries that will not 'grasp the nettle'.

As Martin Cross, Chief Executive, RSA said 'We cannot afford poverty of vision, let alone poverty of aspiration. There are always risks in changing, but the risk of failing to change is much greater.'

**Simon Willis** | Series Editor

DIRECTOR
PUBLIC SECTOR INTERNET BUSINESS SOLUTIONS GROUP
EUROPE, MIDDLE EAST & AFRICA, CISCO SYSTEMS, INC.

Simon Willis came to Cisco after 15 years of work in government and e-business. He has held various senior management and policy positions in the UK government including private secretary to a Minister of State, head of operational reform at the Department of Social Security, head of pensions equalisation and chief executive of a national disability agency. He ran a number of high-level criminal justice and security operations and helped design the new financial services regulatory regime for the UK Treasury.

He also headed numerous UK delegations to the EU, UN and OECD.

After leaving government he worked for a large systems integrator where he focused on IT integration and e-business work, specialising in payment systems, security and market infrastructures. Clients ranged from large European banking groups, through various financial service providers to a variety of European government agencies. Simon Willis has a first class degree in Politics, Philosophy and Economics from Balliol College, Oxford.

**Michelle Selinger** | Editor
EXECUTIVE ADVISER EDUCATION,
CISCO SYSTEMS, EMEA

Michelle Selinger is Executive Adviser Education for Cisco Systems, Europe, the Middle East and Africa. She joined Cisco in 2000 from a background as a teacher and teacher educator. She has a strong research profile with a doctorate from the University of Warwick in the influence of ICT on teaching and learning. She was director of the Centre for New Technologies Research in Education at the University of Warwick prior to joining Cisco. She advises and supports the development of networked based education across the region. She continues to be an active researcher and is regularly invited to contribute to books and journals and to speak at conferences and seminars.

**Shirley Alexander**
PROFESSOR OF LEARNING TECHNOLOGIES AT
THE UNIVERSITY OF TECHNOLOGY, SYDNEY, AUSTRALIA.
DIRECTOR OF THE INSTITUTE FOR INTERACTIVE MEDIA AND LEARNING

One of her major roles is university-wide responsibility for e-learning developments, and she has recently conducted a major evaluation of e-learning across the campus. She has over 15 years' experience in the use of ICT in education, including leading a two-year, national study to evaluate the learning outcomes of 104 e-learning projects, managing the production of numerous e-learning products, and developing and teaching postgraduate courses in multimedia and e-learning. She is currently participating in two nationally funded research projects on the use of e-learning in K-12. She is a member of the Australian Universities Teaching Committee.

**John Anderson**

EDUCATION TECHNOLOGY STRATEGY COORDINATOR,
NORTHERN IRELAND SCHOOL SERVICE, NORTHERN IRELAND.

John Anderson is on secondment from the Department of Education's Education and Training Inspectorate and works for the Education Technology Strategy Management Group which oversees strategy implementation for all education partners in Northern Ireland. He is a member of the British Education Communications and Technology Agency UK government strategy group and of the UK Curriculum Online Content Advisory Board. He is chairman of the Northern Ireland e-Learning Partnership, which brings together all of the partners in the school service to carry out R&D in e-learning and develop the Northern Ireland Virtual School. He has been Adjunct Associate Professor, Duquesne University, Pittsburgh; Deputy Director of the UK Microelectronics Education Programme; Lecturer in Education at the New University of Ulster and Project Officer in the UK's National Development Programme in Computer-Assisted Learning.

**Eddie Brady**

PRINCIPAL, UNITY CITY ACADEMY
ENGLAND.

Eddie Brady has spent 50 years in learning and took up his post as Principal of Unity City Academy in Middlesbrough in January 2002. Prior to this he was head teacher of the Hermitage School in Chester-le-Street, County Durham, from January 1995 to December 2001. Through a combination of enthusiasm and hard work, the Hermitage saw some radical changes. The roll of the school increased dramatically from 720 full-time and no part-time learners in 1994, to being an oversubscribed school with 1000 full-time and 1300 part-time learners. Sixth-form numbers also rose dramatically from 45 in 1104.479 994 to 150 students in 2001. The Hermitage was also included in the HMCI's Report as being a high performing school and one of the most improved in England.

**Andreas Cox**
PROGRAM MANAGER
JORDAN EDUCATION INITIATIVE,
AMMAN, JORDAN.

Andreas Cox is Program Manager, Jordan Education Initiative (JEI), Amman, Jordan. Based in the Ministry of Information and Communications Technology, he is Business Development Manager with CA Computer Associates International and has been seconded to the JEI because of his extensive e-business and e-government consulting background and experience. This has included major engagements with former Eastern European governments in the definition, development and realisation of IT needs in connection with their e-government initiatives. South African born, he graduated in Chemical Engineering from Bradford University, UK in 1987. Based in Germany, Andreas is an Associate Member of the Institute of Chemical Engineers and an active member of the BITKOM Working Group 'Knowledge Engineering and Management' (KEM).

**Marian Brooks**
EXECUTIVE DIRECTOR OF
CAMBRIDGE EDUCATION, ENGLAND.

Marian Brooks is currently Executive Director of Cambridge Education, the leading UK and international provider of educational consultancy and expertise to government agencies, schools and local education authorities. A classroom teacher for 25 years with the last 15 spent as a Principal, she has been closely associated with many of the UK educational reform programmes of recent years. She is a respected contributor to national policy debate and direction and an internationally recognised speaker on a range of educational issues.

**Emile N Cubeisy**
PROGRAM DIRECTOR OF
THE JORDAN EDUCATION INITIATIVE
AMMAN, JORDAN.

Emile N Cubeisy is Program Director of the Jordan Education Initiative (JEI), a partnership between the Government of Jordan, the World Economic Forum, and over 20 of the world's leading corporations. He serves as Advisor on e-initiatives at the Ministry of Information and Communications Technology. Responsibilities include development and support of strategic initiatives empowering Jordanians to use ICT effectively for economic and social development, including the 'Connecting Jordanians Forward Agenda' and management of communications strategies for the spread of a knowledge culture within Jordan. He currently serves on the Board of Trustees of the Princess Sumaya University for Technology. He is a founding member of the International Advertising Association, having served as Vice-President on its Board of Directors, and a founding member of the Young Entrepreneurs Association, a non-profit business association catering to the development of outstanding young entrepreneurs. Born in Lebanon, he graduated from the University of South California and has completed the Senior Executive Program at the Harrow Business School.

**Mark Edwards**
SUPERINTENDENT OF SCHOOLS,
ENRICO COUNTY, VIRGINIA, US.

Mark Edwards has demonstrated tremendous vision and leadership throughout his 25 year career. He began as a science teacher in 1978 and moved up the ranks as an assistant principal, principal and assistant superintendent. He served as superintendent of Danville Public Schools for two years and as Enrico County Public Schools superintendent for ten years. While in Enrico, he put 28,000 laptop computers in the hands of all secondary students and all staff under the nationally known Teaching and Learning Initiative. Dr Edwards was named the Virginia Superintendent of the Year in 2001 and earned the Harold W McGraw Jr Prize in Education, the equivalent of the Pulitzer for the media, in 2003. In July 2004, Edwards became the Dean of the University of North Alabama's nationally accredited College of Education.ern California with a Bachelor in Economics and Political Science and has completed the Senior Executive Program at the Harvard Business School.

**John English**

COMMUNITY SUPERINTENDENT AT
FAIRFAX COUNTY, US.

John English is Community Superintendent at Fairfax County, US.
Before this post, Professor English was a high-school principal, elementary
principal and Metal School associate principal, and served at district level
in schools as assistant superintendent. He attended Dartmouth College,
Johns Hopkins University and University of Virginia; is adjunct professor for
University of Virginia and has done post-doctorate work including at the
Dayton School of Business at the University of Virginia. He describes himself
as a lifelong student.

**François Fillon**

MINISTER FOR NATIONAL EDUCATION,
HIGHER EDUCATION AND RESEARCH
FRANCE.

François Fillon is Minister for National Education, Higher Education and
Research, France. He studied at the University of Maine (Le Mans), René
Descartes University in Paris and the Fondation nationale des Sciences
politiques, and has a masters degree in public law and diploma in applied
public law and political science. He was mayor of Sablé-sur-Sarthe until his
election to Solesme Municipal Council in March 2001. He was elected to
Sarthe General Council (Sablé canton) in 1981 and was its chairman
(1992–98). Since 1998, he has been chairman of the Pays de la Loire
Regional Council; he was deputy in the National Assembly (1981–93) and
was re-elected in 1997 (Rassemblement pour la République (RPR) group).
In 1993 he became Minister of Higher Education and Research in Edouard
Balladur's government, then Minister for Information Technology and the
Post Office in 1995 and was Minister Delegate with responsibility for the
Post Office, Telecommunications and Space (1995–97). In 1998 he became
Spokesman for the RPRs (the political party founded by Jacques Chirac),
before becoming its political adviser (1999–2001). He has been Minister
of Social Affairs, Labour and Solidarity (2002–04) and started a new
governmental mandate in March 2004 as new French Minister for national
education, higher education and research.

## Dmitry Guzhelya

DIRECTOR OF
THE FEDERATION OF INTERNET EDUCATION
RUSSIA.

Dmitry Guzhelya is Director of the Federation of Internet Education (FIE). He started his career as telecommunication network developer about ten years ago and was invited to YUKOS Oil Company to lead the projects on development company networks at Samara and Nefteugansk regions in 1998. He was appointed as one of the directors of the FIE in 2000 when the Federation project was started and is now responsible for the distance teachers training centres development project. He is head of the expert team of Russian Ministry of Education council for ICT in Education.

## Ádám Horváth

IT ADVISER TO
THE MINISTER OF EDUCATION
HUNGARY.

Ádám Horváth is IT adviser to the Minister of Education, Budapest and National member of the e-Learning Committee at the European Commission. He prepares the Educational Informatics Strategy of Education and applies it to the Midterm Development Strategy of Primary and Secondary Education, to the Vocational Strategy, and to the National Development Plan founded by the EU. He is also coordinating the proposal of the Minister to the European Commission to set up a Central European Clearinghouse for online educational content which should break down the barriers (technical, legal, language) of a common market of digital content in the EU. He was previously managing director of Sárga Vonal Kft. (Yellow Line Ltd.); Technical and Financial Manager and Key Account Executive of Graphic Design Studio; and director of the Student Information and Resource Center (Educatio PSC).

**Craig Jones**
STUDENT
SCOTLAND.

Craig Jones is 17 years old (born 3 November 1986) and has lived in Govan, Glasgow most of his life. He writes: 'When I was five years old, I lived with my aunt for a year because my mum was very ill and attended school in Bristol for the my first year of schooling, I then returned to Govan and attended Drumoyne Primary School for six years, later moving onto Govan High School. I plan to go on and study TV Operations and Productions and make a career in this sector. I enjoy playing most sports, especially football, volleyball and rugby. Also I am involved in Space Unlimited (which inspired my career choice!)'

**Ulf Lundin**
DIRECTOR OF
THE EUROPEAN SCHOOLNET
BRUSSELS, BELGIUM.

Ulf Lundin is director of the European SchoolNet. He is responsible for the overall strategy, operation and development of all activities of EUN. Ulf occupies this post after having been the first chairman of EUN from 1997 to 2000. He has worked as State Secretary for Education and Cultural Affairs in Sweden and as Education Counsellor in the Delegation/Permanent Representation of Sweden to the European Union.

**Toine Maes**

GENERAL MANAGER
KENNISNET
THE NETHERLANDS.

Toine Maes is General Manager of Kennisnet. He studied economics at the Tilburg University in the Netherlands. He then started his career as a civil servant within the Ministry of Education and Science and later on within the Ministry of Economic Affairs. In that ministry he was appointed to director of the directorate for technology policy in 1992. In 1997 he became general manager of VECAI, the Dutch umbrella organisation for the cable companies. In February 2001 the Ministry of Education asked him to set up Kennisnet, an independent Internet organisation for the Dutch education sector, and then became its general manager. Kennisnet offers an educational portal and several services to enhance a virtual learning environment.

**David Miliband**

MINISTER OF STATE FOR SCHOOL STANDARDS,
DEPARTMENT FOR EDUCATION AND SKILLS
ENGLAND.

David Miliband was appointed Minister of State for School Standards in June 2002 and has been Labour MP for South Shields since June 2001. He was previously Head of the Prime Minister's Policy Unit (1997–2001) and Head of Policy in the Office of the Leader of the Opposition (1994–97). He was Research Fellow at the Institute for Policy Research (IPPR) (1989–94) and Secretary of the Commission on Social Justice (1992–94). He graduated with First Class Honours in Philosophy, Politics and Economics from Corpus Christi College, Oxford University, and completed a Masters Degree in Political Science at the Massachusetts Institute of Technology, where he was a Kennedy Scholar. He edited Reinventing the Left in 1994, and co-edited Paying for Inequality (also 1994) and was co-founder of the Centre for European Reform. He is President of South Shields Football Club.

**Lyle Oberg**
MINISTER OF LEARNING
ALBERTA, CANADA.

Lyle Oberg is Minister of Learning, Alberta, Canada. He graduated from the University of Alberta in 1983 as a medical doctor and was elected to Alberta's Legislative Assembly in 1993. He served as Minister of Family and Social Services (1997–99) and was then appointed to his current position as Minister of Learning. Under Dr Oberg's leadership, Alberta's learning system has evolved into a more integrated education system with stronger links between the grade-school and post-secondary sectors.

**Kevin Smith**
STUDENT
SCOTLAND.

Kevin Smith is 17. He writes 'My name is Kevin Smith and I live in south side of Glasgow I attended Shawlands Academy Secondary School for four years and I have now left at the age of 16 after completing my Standard Grade exams. I am going on to do my Highers at college and perhaps persue a career in journalism. (If I don't succeed to be a rock'n'roll star!) My interests are in film, music, music and music.'

**Jimmy Stewart**
DIRECTOR OF THE C2K PROJECT
NORTHERN IRELAND.

Jimmy Stewart is Director of the C2K Project, Northern Ireland. He taught Maths and Physics for 13 years at Coleraine Academical Institution before moving to Ballymoney High School as Vice-Principal. In 1988, as head teacher of Ardnaveigh High School, Antrim's first community high school, he was invited to contribute to the development of a specification for a computerised management information system for schools and subsequently served as a member of the procurement team for the Northern Ireland CLASS service. He worked for the CLASS Project as Support Manager in the North Eastern Board area during the 1990s until the establishment of the Classroom 2000 Project (C2K) when he became member of the procurement team. He was appointed Director of Services for C2K in 1999 and now has overall responsibly for delivery and development of this integrated ICT service for all schools throughout Northern Ireland. He has been Associate Lecturer with the Open University since 1987 and has taught a number of modules within their MA course in Educational Management to students across Ireland. He serves on a regional strategy group within BECTA and other strategic groups within Northern Ireland.

**David Triggs**
PRINCIPAL OF
GREENSWARD COLLEGE
ENGLAND.

David Triggs is Principal of Greensward College, Essex, UK, which directly caters for over 1,500 students aged 11–19 and, as a lifelong learning centre, is increasingly offering a range of courses to the wider community under the banner of the University for Industry. Greensward College was the first school in the UK to open a Cisco Regional Academy and now has 45 schools with the network. He has welcomed Tony Blair to Greensward College when Mr Blair launched the e-learning credits system for UK schools. David Triggs has spoken at venues across the UK as well as in the USA, Australia, Russia, Middle East Hong Kong and Sweden. He promoted the need to develop schools as Networked Virtual Learning Organisations. He has been a consultant to various private education companies and worked with schools in seriously challenging circumstance in an effort to enhance the life chances of inners city students. He is committed to working with the UK government and commercial companies to lead the transformation of education.

**Alexander Yu Uvarov**
LEADING RESEARCHER AT
THE SCIENTIFIC COUNCIL OF CYBERNETICS,
ACADEMY OF SCIENCES, RUSSIA.

Alexander Yu Uvarov is the leading researcher (vedushiy nauchniy sotrudnik) at the Research Council on Cybernetics of the Russian Academy of Science. He graduated in educational philosophy from the Russian Academy of Education in 1973, taught high-school students computer science and maths and educational college students conducting research projects. He lead the Informatics Department of Russian Ministry of Education when the first national programme introducing computers into education was started. He was head of the Research Laboratory at the Russian Academy of Science and pro-rector of the University of Russian Academy of Education. He has lead a number of projects in new teacher training methodology, maths and science curriculum development and educational use of ICT. He is a member of the Russian Ministry of Education Expert Council, an expert of the National Training Foundation and member of the Editorial Board of the Informatics and Education Magazine. Dr Uvarov is author/co-author of around 200 publications on the philosophy of education, curriculum development and instructional design, didactics and IT in education.

**Manfred Wolf**
DIRECTOR OF THE INFORMATION TECHNOLOGY DEPARTMENT
CENTRAL INSTITUTE FOR TEACHER TRAINING AND STAFF DEVELOPMENT,
BAVARIA, GERMANY.

Manfred Wolf is Director of the Information Technology Department, Academy of Teacher and Staff Development, Bavaria. He is responsible for planning, organising and evaluating teacher training in the fields of IT and Electrical Sciences for Bavaria (Federal State of Germany) and is national and international coordinator of several education projects including: Training for Trainers in Information Technology; PETRA-Project D82 of the European Commision, 1993–96; Intel® Teach to the Future (with over 200,000 participants in Germany, Austria, Switzerland and South Tirol) since 1999; Cisco Networking Academy Programme (as main contact for 40 Cisco Networking Academies), since 2000; and NET@SCHOOL (qualification of 5400 school system operators), since 2003. He is member of national and international boards including the German–American Dialogue about Media Competency in Education; Bertlesmann Foundation, New York; Guetersloh, 1996–99; Schulen ans Netz (German and European School Net), Bonn, Brussels, 1997–2000; E-Learning-Group of D-21 (21st Century Initiative of the German government), Berlin, since 2000; and German Digita Award of the Best Education Software, Jury, Berlin, since 2001.